"Put down whatever you're reading this very minute and procure this book of lyrics. It'll tug at your heart, or make you laugh, or sing. Sometimes, all at once. Either way, it will shine up any dull moment."
DEE DEE BRIDGEWATER The One and Only

"David is an incredible writer. Any melody you throw at him, he can find words to fit. And he can do it all while having a day job and, no matter what the time difference. The song we wrote together, or should I say, the song he saved me on, 'Ridin' The Bad News Through,' is one of my favorite songs to sing."
CHINA MOSES Singer, Songwriter, Broadcaster

"Greenberg writes lyrics, not music. The thing is, though, you read his lyrics, and you absolutely, sure as day, begin to HEAR the music. You start hearing the melody. You start hearing the harmonies. So it ends up as a collaboration— between Greenberg and you. That's how real, how on the mark, how in-the-pocket his lyrics are."
JONATHAN STONE Former Creative Director, Author of
Moving Day and other novels

"Tape Dave, I could still smell the Glam Seventies in your lyrics. I thought we left that back in High School, but not you."
JED DRAKE Former ESPN Executive Producer, 16-Time
Emmy Award Winner

"Greenberg has always displayed an uncanny gift of observation. You'll find it manifest here in his first book of lyrics. He just needs to find an Elton John to his Bernie Taupin. Perhaps that's you? Whether or not these lyrics sing themselves off the printed page."
CARY BAKER conqueroo (Publicist Extraordinaire)

"Having written music with lyrics in the past, there's a reason why I only write instrumental music now. Reading David's lyrics might lead you to believe that it's child's play, but don't believe it. Do not attempt without adult supervision!"
BOB HOLMES SUSS, Rubber Rodeo

"David Greenberg is a storyteller! He goes deep into the heart and soul of the reader. You can hear music in his words, even if there is no melody behind it, which is a true gift! His play on words, color, and textures graces every page with emotion and grit, but the true surprise is when a walloping laugh pops out of you out of nowhere!"
LUCY WOODWARD Singer, Songwriter, Instructor

MUD FOLIO

{extra sediment edition}

lyrics by

David Greenberg

Beverly · Seattle · Bellagio

a [product] book

ISBN 978-8-9888674-0-1 trade paperback
ISBN 978-8-9888674-1-8 hardcover edition

Printed and distributed through Ingram Spark
10 9 8 7 6 5 4 3 2 1 Czech

Cover design and book typography by Nathan Shumaker
Photography by dG

Additional copyright information can be found on page 279.

mud

Contents

A foreword (of sorts)..xv

...sign dotted line...1
4ever and ever...2
About Love..3
A Day Sublime...5
A Life In The Day (Momentary Glimpses)...6
A Little More Action (for the pimp) 7
Again Sunday/Old Version 9
Again Sunday/Nü Version 10
Alone..11
And Then She Was..13
Among Friends 14
Anything Anytime 15
Arise & Fall Down 16
Asleep Sleeping 18
Baby Blues...19
Baby Said To Say (Another Love Song) 20
Baby's Lament...22
Bad Weather Is Song Writing Time...23
Before You Say Yes..24
Between The Lines 26
Bitches Are Falling..27
Blindness..29
Bobby Don't Give No Damn..30
Bonny, My Havana Holiday...31
Bourbon Sheets 33
But My Mama...34
Bye Goodbye...35
Casanova 36
Can I Keep It Up...37
Catch A Fire...39
Cathy Said 40
Cousin Bob Wears Tennis Shoes...41
Cross That Line...42

Dangerous Findings 44

Dear Sir 45

Do We Know Any Allman Bros.? 48

Don't Drink My Beer Buddy Polka 50

Drip Dry 51

Dropping 53

Electric Appliance Day 54

Endings 56

Everything (love song nr. 85) 58

Evolution 59

Faery 61

Farewell 62

Feets Move 63

Floating 65

Ford Gone So Mad 67

Galdino Pataxo Warrior 69

Go For Broke 70

Get Back In The Back Seat 72

Going Back 73

Gone 75

Grind 'Em Till You Find 'Em 76

Hands Down 78

Heaven Can Wait 79

He's A Bitch 80

Here2There 82

Hey Hey New Jersey (Greetings From Ozone Park) 84

In This Place 86

I'm Not Talking 87

I'm The Baby You're Having 88

Is It Hot In Here? 89

I've Got Plenty (Of Nothing) 91

It's Only How You Said (Compensation) 92

Jump 94

Just Another Bar Band 96

Just Need Love 98

Keeping Amused 100

The King Of Rock & Roll 102

The Last Time (Let's Pretend) 103

Lead Me On 104

Leaves Change 106

Left Ear 108

Letter From China (Rock 2-4).. 109

Live A Little..111

Looking For Some 113

Love Is A Many Splintered Thing 114

Love, Love, Love...115

Low Rent Rhumba (The)...117

LNFS (Superdupermarket Remix)...119

Miami Heat..120

Miracle Mile..121

Morning Before Sunrise 123

Mousie 124

MRI 125

Mud 126

Mumm's The Word..128

New Day Drowning..129

Night Club... 131

No Bikini Atoll..132

Nothing Left 133

Not Moving 134

No Way Nothing...135

Now/Then 136

On Catsteps..137

On Parade..138

On The Road 140

On Top 141

One More Rung.. 143

One Way (In The Tunnel) 144

The Peon Dance 146

The People-People..147

People Person 149

Philo-Sophie... 151

Pimms!..152

Pick Up Stix.. 154

The Policeman's Polka... 156

Political Song nr. 24 157

The Pressure Scheme 158

Questions I Forgot (To Ask)..159

The Ragman.. 161

Rape.. 163

Rewind (Waste A Rhyme) 164

Remotely Unseen.. 166

Ridin' The Bad News Through..167

Road Kill...169

Sad Café...170

Scratch That 7yr Itch..171

See You..172

Sending Out Signals...174

Sexting...175

She Still Says No!..177

Shooby Dooby Moon...178

Silent Night..180

Sky Babies..181

Sleep Tight...183

Sneaker Love..184

Something For Nothing...185

So Much Better Than That..187

Sour Lime...189

Springtime in December...191

Stardance...192

The Stars Smile The Wind Laughs.......................................193

Strange Agents On The Assembly Line.................................195

Strangers No More..197

Stuck In Reverse...199

Suddenly..201

Sunglasses For Peter: The Installation Party........................203

The Sun Glides...205

Supposin' To Be A Constitution (Protest saong Nr. 12)..........206

TeeVee, Dinner, Table, Chair & Stove..................................208

Talk To Plants...209

Them Track Star Blues..211

These People Here Need You..212

They Slept In Tents (Old Version)..213

They Wonder Why Things Don't Change...............................214

This Night Wounds Time...216

Throbbing Funk..217

Too To Do...218

Traveled Too Far...220

True Blue..222

True Fax (At The Stop & Shop)...224

The Truth About It All...225

Uh Oh Oh No..227

Upa War Jazz..228

Vegetable Blues 230
Venus De Mellow 231
Walking Hat..232
Wasting Time At Maureen's..233
Wet Smiles Of A Summer Night..235
We've Got The Power 236
What Do Boys Want?..237
What I Want..239
What You Want...241
Why Are You Staring At Me? 243
Why You Can't Load The Dishwasher Dear 244
Wind (the sound of crying) 246
Words For Everything...248
Wrong Kind of Sorry..250
Yet We Dare..252
You Promised..254
You'll Remember Me 255
You're Not Jesus Or Jesus Saves (Plaid Stamps) 257
You're One..258
Zero-Zero-One-One-Two..260

The Machine Gun Rag
Ahh, yes this...261
I Informal Interview...262
II The Siamese Libidinous Navy (Or Anchors Aweigh Tania) 266
III Peppermint Patty & The Tapes..267

As to the order of things..269
About the author..275
Oh no, there's more..277
Additional Copyright Info..279
Non-exclusive license (to thrill)...281

A foreword (of sorts)

David Greenberg has been writing lyrics since before he could crawl. Not really, but it seems that the general public falls entranced into submission by enfants of all shapes, sizes, demeanors, and especially those touting misdemeanors. Since I needed to hook you, the reader, a dues-paying member of the general public, I decided to stoop very low into reading this author's note. Terribly low.

I usually flip past this page, past the foreword written to add perspective and stuffing between the lines. The bulk of the book, what I plunked down my good money for, is what I want to read straight away. I can bring my perspective to the reading, and anyway, what does the author really know about how I understand their book? The author's only birthed the words, only laboriously pushed them out for all the world to see. It's a great deal of work, to-be-sure. I'm not belittling that—or to giving birth—much the opposite, but there is significantly much more to the experience of a book than writing it, and that is the act of readers reading it.

In the reader's mind is where the characters breathe, where the essay provokes thought, questions, and answers and pride and anger, hate and love, where you can feel Calvin being trounced by Hobbes. What does the author know about that? He can only imagine, and even then, his/her/their imagination is not large enough to contain the universe of possibilities the world of readers can bring to the material. Even Watterson cannot know how hard, and often, I can make Calvin bounce off the walls; badabing bamboom kerash! So I push forward into the book, jump into the thick of it, straightaway.

It is good to plunge directly into prose, but what lies ahead for you in this book are lyrics. Most of which have never had as much as a note of music written for them. No singers have strung the words together to float them in the air, suspended aloft by melodies. The words lie dormant on the pages waiting to be read and, better yet, sung. I tried to hook you into reading this preface as some minor explanations are needed to explain the why of this book of lyrics-never-yet-sung.

I write lyrics.

I don't write music.

Between those two statements lies the rub.

The ideas come to me, and I need to write them down whenever I could find paper, immediately, or they could vanish into nothingness again. I remember sitting in a parking lot, late for a party, writing the lyrics to "Cathy Said" by the dimming light of my dashboard. Good thing the words came quickly, or else my elderly VW Bug would have needed a jump-start. Now I consider that real creative pressure. The bands in grammar, junior, and high school that I hung around with were guys, always guys, who only played at dances covering the best of LedZep, Marshall Tucker, Cream, Santana, Tull—no originality allowed at this music scene. If the dancers couldn't dance to it, you were beaten to a bloody pulp.

Okay, okay, this was suburbia...perhaps pummeled by tennis rackets was more like it. I did try to make it easy for the boys in the band by writing a parody of "My Woman From Tokyo," one of the top tunes of the time within the ditty of "Cousin Bob Wears Tennis Shoes." There was no twinkle of recognition, not even a tune-up of the guitars to have a pathetic and uninspired go at it. Weird Al had not invented himself yet, so parody was just a joke and not a business model.

The lyrics have since stayed silent in my notebooks. It was not much better when I was a roadie for the band Road Apple, which later signed onto the Vanguard label as Flying Island. They played fusion, instrumental flights of jazz-rock. I kept at it anyway. The words kept rhyming, sort-of, and the stanzas formed images and became ponderous stories sometimes as I experimented with wordplay. (It wasn't the drugs believe me...remember, I was around musicians after all. I never inhaled! Not too much, at least.) The band read most of my neatly typed up pages at breaks.

One song even provoked a comment.

Dave, these songs are too long.

That one clocked in at five pages. I had a lot to say in those days, or at least a lot of words in which to say it. On the spot, I wrote my ode to Max Ernst, "Walking Hat." At seven lines, it's a dry spit of lyric. They liked it, reminded me they were an instrumental band and stayed that way until they imploded (after two all-instrumental albums) for all the usual career-impeding reasons. You and I can fill in the blanks as I never delved into their problems after I went off to college. I had my own and ripped them apart and taped them back into songs.

I had high hopes for these suckers. I even thought one of them, "Sky Babies," would be a great hit for David Bowie or any other Glam Rockers then shining on during the 1970s. As a high schooler in the 'burbs, I had no contacts with any A-list managers or publishers or agents. No amount of wishing was gonna get the pages into an envelope and addressed to...who knew who or where? Even so, I put the chorus of that song into my high school quote with the faint idea that, perhaps, thirty years later, I would have had the right contacts, and all my classmates would look at my quote and think...*right on, cool, I remember that hit song. Where is Greenberg now?* Unfortunately, no one did anything with the lyrical, except for me putting the chorus where it definitely couldn't make any sense to anyone at all. Then, and most certainly now, I am sure it still causes head-scratching and general befuddlement.

That is, if anyone does happen to stop at my picture in the yearbook to wonder *what the heck ever happened to that guy? Still strange after all these years?* More famous dudes and dudettes in the NCHS class of 1974 warrant a second thought, so maybe a puff, or a piffle, of a wonder sent my way.

I've added much to the folio, with just a scant wee bit of the lyricals tweaked and twisted into songs through the decades since. It probably has to do with the words coming before the music, and most musicians I have known create the other way around.

Another reason may be my experimentation, or my verbosity, or the fact that I don't write music. My punctuation may not consistently fit any kind of meter or musical schematic. Or perhaps the lyrics were too far ahead of their time, or behind their time, or just out of time altogether.

I know they don't totally suck. At least not as much as the hundreds of bad demos I heard while part of the A&R team at Rykodisc, or like some of the thousands of so-called pop songs played on Top 40 radio after I became aware of the fact that people got paid silly amounts of money to write little silly words to silly little love songs. I love a good pop song, which is why the bad ones playing on heavy rotation are so punishingly sad and brutally painful to this boy's ears and hapless soul. It could've been one of mine. Part of mine, at least.

My hope is this: since these lyricals have been gathered and polished and made available for reading by this edition of the *Mud Folio*, they will also be re-edited by the musicians who will write the melodies and sung by the singers who will breathe life into the songs for the audiences who will live through them, or by them, or hum them while doing chores. That is the reason for publishing this thing, this *Mud Folio*. This is the ticket to ride for all the lyrics still clinging to the safety of my notebooks. This is my act of kicking them out of the house.

Yo, guys! Guys, this is graduation day.

All my enfants, I wish you well and some hard-earned good luck, and when you do get a paying job, please send some money home through BMI, which is where the Tape Dave Music Co. gathers the pennies before the accountants ship them to us up here on the North Shore of Massachusetts.

Thanks to Sarah Williams and Michael Epstein for word processing my hand-scrawled lyrics from the well-worn notebooks, and through their unintentional revisions—a.k.a. typos—they made me take a new look at the old stuff.

I initially wrote this foreword without giving thanks to anyone, even though a very many deserve it. So, after giving thanks to the two who did the heavy lifting of typing, a whole boatload of names drifted into view, and then, the thanking grew into something of spectacular proportions. This is not a book of great importance to the world which owes so many appreciations to be imparted. It's just a slim book of lyrics, unsung ones at that, and going on and on and on started to look ridiculous.

So I ripped them all out.

Sorry to you all who might have been looking as your name has also not made it into this, Volume Dos of Mud, the extra sediment edition. Oh well, maybe some other piece of writing worthy of a substantial thank you list in the near to distant future will allow some credit to be given? Maybe. Probably not, as even an ordinary-sized novel cannot be found in my head these days, let alone one that could allow so many "thank yous" to be given.

Three names, though, needed to be reinserted. The three teachers who energized my creativity along the way: Ron and Nancy Russell-Tutty, who prodded, cajoled, and sparked my imagination at New Canaan High School and Joel Savishinsky, Ph.D., who did the same at Ithaca College and during our fieldwork on Cat Island, the Bahamas. Of course, to the Moms and Dads on both sides of the aisle (Beverly and Sydney, Emily and Erwin) and all the family and friends who've loved, helped, nurtured, and inspired me this far and who will most assuredly do so in the future, thank you.

Those others on the opposite side of the street—most obviously not the sunny side—those who have beaten me up emotionally, darkened my days, and rendered more than a few nights sleepless, many thanks are due here as well. Your turn of the screw helped me craft some of the songs I hold most dear.

Although blithely moving on, you most probably don't know who you are and hopefully, never will, but thanks none-the-less. Like Jack Webb intoned on the old TeeVee show, *Dragnet,* the names have been changed. Not to protect the innocent mind you, more like allowing me to hide behind the fictions.

And not get pummelled by tennis rackets.

Like my life, this book is supremely dedicated to Laurie for being there, to Mia and Tess for arriving via amazingly different routes—neither mode of which has anything to do with how each of you is my favorite—to Trixie, we miss your thumperousness, to Sadie we miss you as well for all your doggedly blind love and devotion, and to them all for putting up with me.

David Greenberg
...with one foot and half a heart in NYC and the rest in
Beverly, MA.

I first wrote that bit about allowing part of me to metaphorically linger back in New York City many years ago when I first started to compile these lyrics, and both sets of parents were still alive. Now it's more like both feet are firmly up here, and those fond memories of the Manhattan-era are brightly polished up and smoothed out of most of the rough patches, dingy spots, and hard times we lived through before we begrudgingly(!) moved out. And, may you forever rest in peace, Emily and Syd and Beverly and Trixie and Sadie.

This edition includes some thirty-two new lyrics: the extra sediment, if you will. Some were written to music, one written to music whose audio file has disappeared, possibly written over, but definitely not here, there, or anywhere. The others? As usual, they are lyrics-never-sung, still waiting for their music to be composed, their chance at the microphone, the vowels held breathless for a few seconds, when appropriate, the thoughts within clarified with added emotion, their implied rhythms ignited.

max ernst:
"watch your hat!"

…sign dotted line…

You sounded cold as if you were freezing
Was something wrong I felt like asking
Across the thousand wires
Into the air
I wanted to ask
But for some reason I didn't dare

You liked the present
As if it were heaven sent
"Dynamite" as if it exploded
The note itself was loaded

Through the mist I crept
Passed a couple of locked doors
Behind them hetero mates waged their
Primal instinct combative wars

What was it that was wrong
You sounded cold as if you were freezing
Was something wrong I felt like asking
Over the thousand wires
Over the phone
It felt impersonal
Now divorced completely
From the calcium deflected Hell
Was something wrong
I didn't bother to ask

4ever and ever

(Background smoothie chorus sings: Girl)

Telling me what you have in mind
Telling me what you have in store
But don't take up all of my time, don't waste it
Your questions can be such a bore

(Girl)

Seems like you have made up your mind
Decided to give me a tough enough time
A tough love I don't mind, just hate to waste it
On a talk talk talking girl who whines

(Chorus:)
You can talk (Girl) 4ever (and ever and ever and ever)
But (Girl) you'd better find another lover
Who's patient enough to wait (Girl)
To wait forever to get you (Girl) under the covers
'Cause 4ever's just too long for me

(4ever's too long)
(4ever's too long)
(4ever and ever and ever)
(Girl)

Don't have that much time to spend
Spent all my time so far to fit yours
Time now for another lover, I can taste it
Unless you change that line of yours

(Chorus here of "4ever and ever and ever Girl" going 4ever)

About Love

Starve a cold feed a fever put a sprain in a sling
When you're hungry you'll eat almost anything

But what about love

If it's deadly and toxic you find a vaccine
Google that word if you don't know what it means

But what about love

It's a problem without a solution (That's what about love)
One of the disasters of evolution (That's what about love)
Mind over matter matters a lot (That's what about love)
Love always finds my weakest spot (That's what about love)
If looks could kill I'm a dying man (That's what about love)
Love is war and I don't have a plan (That's what about love)

If love is the drug what's this freaking disease
Punched me in the gut got me down on my knees

So what
About love

The joy of sex in one night stands I loved the casual fling
When she's gone I feel lost whole lotta nothing

So what
About love

It's a solution without a problem (That's what about love)
Life's joke that seems so random (That's what about love)
From heaven above that's quite a fall (That's what about love)
You don't mind nothing matters at all (That's what about love)
Got you wrapped in her angel wings (That's what about love)
Brace yourself for love's sweet sting (That's what about love)

There's no gain in this pain I've bottomed out

She's got that everything I can't do without
That's what about love
From the pit of despair to the heavens above
She's got that thing the Devil calls love
She's got that thing the Devil calls love
That's about all the love I can take

That's the what about love

A Day Sublime

(Lyrics fashioned to the melody of "A Love Supreme" by John Coltrane.)

My love supreme
(And) my life divine
(And) a light to read
The hidden path
Will make my day
A day sublime
A day sublime
A day sublime
A day sublime

(And) now to find
The way to now
To make my love
A love supreme
A love supreme
A love supreme
A love supreme

The sun goes down
(And) the life I lead
Under a broken sky
Is a life divine
A life divine
A life divine
A life divine

Supreme supreme
A day sublime
Sublime sublime
A life divine
(etcetera and on through fade out)

A Life In The Day (Momentary Glimpses)

The day opens with a cloudless sunrise
Yourself a wandering soul with child feet
Checking notes removing your tie
Then relaxing on a wall trying to sleep

Sit up with harmless surprise
Visually refraining from taking too much in
People move—pawns in a medieval fight
Shoving attacking moving so far away

The sky now collaged with cotton balls
Sentinels of the wind
Clouds returning from the fall
Sentinels of the wind

Shadows impressions against stone
Momentary glimpses
People returning personally alone
Momentary glimpses

Pawns and lawns and workaday afternoons
Does it all add up or does it multiply
Or does it cut to the quick and signify doom
And you fall to sleep not wanting to try

The night now full of deep darkness
Silent and watching
No moon no stars doubting sadness
Silent and watching

Shadows impressions against stone
Momentary glimpses
People returning personally alone
Momentary glimpses

A Little More Action (for the pimp)

Played with people toyed with lives
Mangled measly little souls

Usually a working out of ideals
Usually mine deciding who and what
In a backward way I got my way
Not with force did it with my eyes shut

I played with people
Pulling them my way
Then letting go
And watching them
With nothing left to say
Letting them die
Ever so slow

I played with people
Toying with their dreams
Playing and changing
And finally rewriting
What it was they thought it means
Blinding their minds
Mostly rearranging

I thought I was playing the Devil
Using people as if they were under Contract
I found out I was the child
Indifferent trying to own when I felt detached

Just toys in my hand
I owned them I owned you
Acting out my demands
Giving me all I was due

I played with people
Pulling them my way
Then letting them go

And watching them
With nothing left to say
Letting them die
Ever so slow

I thought I was playing God
Using people as if they were under my thumbs
I found out I was just a babe

Indifferent trying to get out from feeling so dumb
I thought I was God
Crushing people under my thumbs
Just a just a just a simpleton idiot
Running away from all you can run away from

I owned them I owned you
Give me all I am due
I owned them I owned you
Give me all I am due
I owned them I owned you
Give me all I am due

I played with people
Pulling them apart
Then letting go
I played with people
I toyed with lives
They held me down
They let me go

Again Sunday/Old Version

Again Sunday again Sunday again Sunday
It is Sunday and it is Sunday and it is Sunday and
I've taken up my pen again

Monday Tuesday Wednesday Thursday Friday Saturday
It is Sunday and it is Sunday and it is Sunday and
I've let time go soft and bend

Again Sunday again Sunday again Sunday
A Tuesday if it was a Tuesday if it was a Tuesday if it was
Sondra'd have my letters to send

Monday Tuesday Wednesday Thursday Friday Saturday
It is Sunday and it is Sunday and it is Sunday and
I've taken up my pen again

I'm drawing fine lines
I'm drawing fine lines
I'm drawing fine lines
The fine lines of poetry

Sondra's listening to me
Sondra's thinking of me
Sondra's half asleep
Laughing half-heartedly

Again Sunday again Sunday again Sunday
Monday Tuesday Wednesday Thursday Friday Saturday
It is Sunday and it is Sunday and it is Sunday
(Etcetera on through to ending fade)

Again Sunday/Nü Version

Again Sunday again Sunday again Sunday
It is Sunday and it is Sunday and it is Sunday and
I've taken up my pen again

Monday Tuesday Wednesday Thursday Friday Saturday
It is Sunday and it is Sunday and it is Sunday and
I've let time go soft and bend

Again Sunday again Sunday again Sunday
A Tuesday if it was a Tuesday if it was a Tuesday if it was
I'd have some letters to send

Again Sunday again Sunday again Sunday
It is Sunday and it is Sunday and it is Sunday and
I've taken up my pen again

I'm drawing fine lines
I'm drawing fine lines
I'm drawing fine lines
The fine lines of poetry
The fine lines around my sanity
The fine lines of conversation
The fine lines around you and me

I'm not listening to me
I'm not thinking of me
I'm just half asleep
Laughing half heartedly

Again Sunday again Sunday again Sunday
It is Sunday and it is Sunday and it is Sunday and
I've taken up my pen again

Alone

Loneliness stirs
A snake whispers
Darkness surrounds as the night scrapes the ground

Loneliness stirs
A cat's paw tearing at a pane of glass
Its sound sends shivers and shards up my backbone
Tearing at my seemingly sleepy mind awaking

Loneliness stirs
A snake whispers through blades of grass
Bending the pawns of the wind
Who kneel when the wind is attacking

A song in the wind echoes
Over emptied miles of darkened sea houses
While the surf's pounding and gripping
The army of sea rocks tearing and destroying

Darkness surrounds
As the night scrapes the ground
As I sit staring at my window
While music comes blaring out the radio

The light's turned off
And the room sits in shadows
Loneliness stirs
As the shutters are wrenched in their hinges
Porch chairs
Of summer days are blown about
Loneliness stirs
While the feeling of being lonely jumps to shout

Cat tearing shutters crashing
The surf pounding at the shore
While listening to the whispering
Of the wind blowing across the floor

Night scraping time delaying
While sitting in my only chair
Asking do I really care

Loneliness stirs
A snake scraping
Darkness surrounds as the night devours the ground

And Then She Was

And then she was
And then she was
And then she

And then she said
You can sleep alone tonight
And then she said
Don't throw away this fight

And then she turned
As if a photograph
And then she turned
And laughed her goodbye laugh

And then she left
Pulled down in her undertow
And then she left
With all I would never know

And then she was
And then she was
And I am

Written to track by Sawandi Simon—though said track has been lost to either overwriting of the hard drive or slid into the trashcan folder or just somewhere else with no map as to where that could be. Whichever way it went is wondrously par for the sand-trappy course my lyric writing putters upon.

Among Friends

She was among friends
Till those friends decided it was time to end
She loved them all
Till they decided to make her take a fall
And she slipped away

She needed a port of no return
For she had no "where" to turn
Looking around she faltered
She had no one left to call to her
And say I love you

(Chorus:)
Now she's idle as a streamlined Chevrolet
Do what you want but don't get in her way
She may be your pet but you may be her prey
She smiles
You're among friends so say what you want to say

She says so coolly
But she listens to your every word
Laughing slightly
But she doesn't warm to what she's heard
She doesn't love you

(Chorus)

I like her style
She just takes time just a little while
To understand her
But right now you have to unhand her
I'll take my time
I'll take my time
I'll take my time

(Chorus)

Anything Anytime

(Female:)
Been sitting here all alone
Hoping you would call me on the phone
Let your fingers do the walking (and call me up)
And we'll end up talking

Call me (anytime anyplace) / Call me (anytime anyplace)
Call me anything anything you want
Call me (anytime anyplace) / Call me (anytime anyplace)
Call me anytime anyplace anything / Call me please

(Male:)
Been thinking of calling you tonight
This dark night surely needs your light
And I have to smooth over the lies
I told you once and I told you twice

Call me (anytime anyplace) / Call me (anytime anyplace)
Call me anything anything you want
Call me (anytime anyplace) / Call me (anytime anyplace)
Call me anytime anyplace anything / Call me please

(Both:)
Don't think I can wait it out
Can't wait another minute
Our falling in and falling out
I'll even let you win it

Call me (anytime anyplace) / Call me (anytime anyplace)
Call me anything anything you want
Call me (anytime anyplace) / Call me (anytime anyplace)
Call me anytime anyplace anything / Call me please

Perhaps a signature tune for an Off-Off Broadway musical? Or I could license it for a wireless service advert? Yeah, that's the ticket. Then I can trade the rights for an infinite upgrade and really get more bars in all the forgotten places.

Arise & Fall Down

Rising falling / Rise and falling
Arise and fall down / Rise and falling

When you get up do you have to fall down
Can't you sit still do you have to move around
Constant moving hey you're getting on my nerves
Bottom of the barrel is just what you deserve

Rising falling / Rise and falling
Arise and fall down / Rise and falling

Afraid to stay on the top of the heap
Arise and fall down try to land on your feet
When you're hurt don't come running to me
Go down and out it's a safe place to be

Rising falling / Rise and falling
Arise and fall down / Rise and falling

King of the hill can't keep your crown
If you're lying face down on the ground
Least you could be is homeward bound
Get up step lively you just fall down

Rising falling / Rise and falling
Arise and fall down / Rise and falling / Rising / Falling

Rising falling / Rise and falling
Arise and fall down / Rise and falling

When you get up do you have to fall down
Bury your face in the cold cold ground
Down and out is the safer place to be
Than to try and stand on your own two feet

Rising falling / Rise and falling
Arise and fall down / Rise and falling

Afraid to stay on the top of the heap
Arise and fall down can't land on your feet
Bottom of the barrel is not what you deserve
Stand tall forge ahead steel your nerves

Rising falling / Rise and falling
Arise and fall down / Rise and falling

When you stand tall people will put you down
Lock you up when you want to go to town
Can't be king of the hill if you're flat on your face
Pull yourself up until it's the wind that you taste

Rising falling / Rise and falling
Arise and fall down / Rise and falling

Arise the fallen it's the clouds you embrace
Arise the fallen wrap your arms around grace
Arise the fallen go ahead tempt the fates
Arise the fallen it's never too late
Arise the fallen don't pause don't wait
Arise the fallen dust off your charity plate
Arise the fallen give your greatest wealth
Arise the fallen give all of your self
Arise the fallen give until weightless
Arise the fallen

Asleep Sleeping

Squatting on the corner;
Sweater, pea jacket; and his mad dog
Spilled on his coat.

Detested with his situation;
Stinking, sweating, on a windy day;
Blowing his hair around.

His eyes all cataract blue;
Deaf and, dumb and blind, and asleep.
Sprawled on the sidewalk.

The Mad Dog twenty-twenty
Falls off, and down, onto the pavement
Dyeing the cement red; blood.

Asleep—sleeping; trying to fritter away,
His mind doesn't remember to say:
"I want to live/love, today."

Asleep—sleeping; deaf to life's calling.
He drinks only to keep stalling
The past from catching up.

Squatting in his stool;
Eyes red, nose dripping, mouth drooling
Spilling on his coat.

The heat and lights spark out.
His shadow, and his eyes, remain staring
Etched into my brain.

Asleep—sleeping; in his low chair.
Asleep—sleeping; sucking his on his bottle.
Asleep—sleeping; the sunset of his eyes etched onto my brain.

Baby Blues

Stick my feet in a bucket of cement
Take away my money can't pay the rent
Don't even ask if my love is true
I just melt when I see those baby blues
Baby blues, baby blues
I just melt when I see those baby blues
Nothing I can honestly do
I just melt when I see those baby blues

Keep you safe from the cold cruel world
Keep you safe my little little girl
Don't even think that my love ain't true
I'm just inflicted with those baby blues
Baby blues, baby blues
I'm just inflicted with those baby blues
Nothing I can honestly do
I'm just inflicted with those baby blues

Inflict me baby

Give you love a picket fence and a lawn
Be damn sure a new day'll always dawn
Do it alone if I really have to
Start right now to wash away them blues
Baby blues, baby blues
I just melt when I see those baby blues
Nothing I can honestly do
I'm just inflicted with those baby blues

Baby Said To Say (Another Love Song)

Baby asked again if I love her
Baby's getting suspicious
Groundwork we have to recover
Oh baby's ugly sickness

She said to say I love you   (I love you, I love you, I love
She said to say it a thousand times   you, I love you, I love you, I
She said to say I love you   love you, etc. & on)
And every other word that rhymes
Baby said to say I love you
But say it differently
Say yea (yea)
Say ahweeooooo (ahweeoooo)
Say damdiddlywon (damdiddlywon)
Say sazzleedo (sazzleedo)

She said that yes she did

Baby said if I love her to prove it
I guess I have to go
All the way as she's planned it
Then we'll have all the way to go

She said to say I love you   (I love you, I love you, I love
She said to say it a thousand times   you, I love you, I love you, I
She said to say I love you   love you, etc. & on)
And every other word that rhymes
Baby said to say I love you
But say it differently
Say yea (yea)
Say ahweeoooo (ahweeoooo)
Say damdiddlywon (damdiddlywon)
Say sazzleedo (sazzleedo)

(AUDIENCE PARTICIPATION TIME and repeat the "ahweeoooos" and
"damdiddlywons" and whatever else is necessary to make this one
damn fine ditty suitable for play on the radio station of your choice.

If that's a country station, by all means twang it up and add in all the "dangs" ya got. If emo, just slur the words and drop the beat to a dirge and perhaps change the background chorus to "I like you, maybe, I think." The use of parentheses usually denotes where I would like the words as sung by the background chorus, unless it is an instruction like this is and instructions are not usually sung by any reasonably sane person, except maybe in the odd, Off-off Broadway avant-garde musical. One, two, three, go make this a commercial hit song...now! I have bills to pay and places to go and people to meet who want me to pay for their coffee before they'll let me write their damn script!)

She said to say I love you
She said to say it a thousand times
She said to say I love you
And every other word that rhymes
Baby said to say I love you
But say it differently
Say yea (yea)
Say ahweeooooo (ahweeoooo)
Say damdiddlywon (damdiddlywon)
Say sazzleedo (sazzleedo)

(I love you, I love you, I love you, I love you, I love you, I love you, etc. & on)

Baby's Lament

I've been down
I've been out
I've been most places you've never been
A broken man
See me fall
Nobody's ever getting under this skin

Chew me up
Spit me out
How does it taste, your Last Supper?

\

Written for an especially poignant scene centered around the evil protagonist of my musical film script, *Sticks & Stones*. S&S was/is a spec script meant to be my ticket out of the below-the-line life I was leading at the time and move on up to the creative side of the film business. Says a lot that I have worked in the music business for the last thirty-plus years after I finished the script and solicited agents galore. But who's counting? Okay, little devil guy sitting on my shoulder, I get it. You can stop now.

Bad Weather Is Song Writing Time

Should we talk about the children
Or the neighbors and the things they say
Loose lips so determined
To cheer us through our lonely days

Should we talk about the weather
Should we talk about the mess you made
Should we do this together
Or should we go our separate ways

Should we talk this through
Or should we throw some things
This is nothing new
So I'd rather throw some things

My love's been scorched pride's been burned lightning strikes
   and pitted by hail
The ice storm has come and gone floodwaters have overturned
No living room beds washed away it just goes on and on and on

You fell in deep
And way too far
She jumped right in
And you let her
So, yes,
Let's talk about the weather

Before You Say Yes

Lift up your veil
I want to remember how beautiful you are now
Not the way we were

Just look at you
Perfect from head to toe such a blushing bride and your
Curves still swerve

Can he love you more than I did back when our dreams
              barely kept us alive
We were so young without a care in the world
A dangerous little boy and a scared little girl
You've won it big and then some you make it easy to justify
Leaving you with alibis

Before you say yes
Before you say yes
And leave for your mansion on the hill
Before you say yes remember I did love you
I always have and I always will

Hot damn honey
Even months on the road your looks could kill for sure
Boys came unglued

Town after town
I had to fight every drunk who wanted into your pants
So deja true (or: that's so damn true)

Can he love you more than I did back when our dreams
              barely kept us alive
We were so young without a care in the world
A dangerous little boy and a scared little girl
We were crushed by our dreams and schemes and near misses
And then things got vicious

Before you say yes

Before you say yes
Let me swallow pride's bitter little pill
Before you say yes remember I did love you
I always have and I always will

(Bridge)
Paper plates plastic forks and a bottle of Heinz
And your tricks of love helped us loose our minds
Who cares which side the little spoon even goes on
When it was all we could do to keep our clothes on
Don't give me those airs of a dilettante
I know what you need still got what you want

How I failed
To understand what I needed was more than half a chance
With a lover like you

One last kiss please
I want to remember how wonderful you are now
Least I deserve

Can he love you more than I did back when our dreams barely kept us alive
We were so young without a care in the world
A dangerous little boy and a scared little girl
I wish you well with your new life of leisure
All that cold-blooded pleasure

Before you say yes
Before you say yes
Warm me up with a hug and a smile instead of this chill
Before you say yes
Before you say yes
Before you say yes
And lock yourself in to that mansion on the hill
Before you say yes remember I did love you
I always have and I always will

Between The Lines

Read between the lines
It's not black and white not grey nothing at all
Read between the lines
It's as empty as it is wide as it is tall
Read between the lines
You can fill it with most anything at all
Hate, love, darkness, or light
What would you rather tote around
Hate, love, darkness, or light
Flying high, grovel on the ground
Read between the lines
What you don't say, that speaks to me
Read between the lines
What you don't do, is what I tend to see
Read between the lines
What I mean is what you mean to me
Hate, love, darkness, or light
What would you rather tote around
Hate, love, darkness, or light
Flying high, grovel on the ground

I went to see theSHIFT play in a small club in the middle of New Hampshire. I was going to write in the middle of Nowhere, NH, but that didn't seem fitting as this was definitively somewhere where fans of good live music live, having decided, on a Sunday night no less, to check on these guys. theSHIFT don't play your usual rock songs, more intellectual, though with flowing vibes, so to be a fan of theirs is not a slam-dunk, you betcha: you will have to do more than just nod to the beat and regurgitate the lyrics; you will have to connect to the long and guarded souls of the songs. Here is a song that I had hoped John Shannon would lay his luxe melodies into, and then, with MJ Lambert and Benjamin Geis, remember to play it when they started playing those arenas. Years later, the band changed their name to Leaders Of The Shift, then since it has taken that long to proof this sucker, they survived the pandemic and have returned as theSHIFT. Yet so far, they have not emerged out of Clubland. Too bad, they deserve better.

Bitches Are Falling

(toppling of the powers that be inna pop song....
cos for sure...money makes the world go round
until it all comes tumbling down)

(Chorus:)
bitches are falling bitches are falling
bitches are falling bitches are falling
bitches are falling all over town
look down on us with noses in the air
bitches are falling i don't care
why do you

bitches are falling
bad ass 'tudes and tight little frowns
serves em right they're going down

bitches are falling
spoiled fat rat bastard husbands
la dolce vita il duce demands

bitches are falling
let us eat cake and sugar and fat
they take and take let's get it back

(Chorus here)

bitches are falling
canapés in their towers of power
throw us leftovers after they sour

bitches are falling
sweet noses and perfect those asses
blud diamonds in blingifed sunglasses

bitches are falling
bad ass 'tudes and tight little frowns
serves em right they're going down

down down down uptown downtown they're going down
money makes the world go round but what goes up must

all over town bitches are bitching
those big wheel heels they're going down

bitches are falling
privileged and arrogant
love you darling now get bent

bitches are falling
trim little noses whip lashing tongues
get out the hoses let's have us some fun

(Chorus here too)

Misheard a song on the radio and had to Shazam it to see if it really was "bitches are falling" or not. Because if it wasn't, I sure was going to try and write a song around that nugget of a phrase. Shazam I did, and was well on my way to another Tape Dave lyrical. What I misheard was close in sound but not in verbiage or attitude. So, in between stoplights and stop-and-go traffic—which was endemic on my way through Boston to that music booking workplace in Brighton whose shall still not be named—I popped down some ideas and rhymes and schemes and littered the floor of my car with them.

Blindness

Blindness come come over me
Keep me forever in the dark / No more sun no sun to warm
Warm to unfreeze my heart

There goes my girl with her new boy
Don't wanna see her / Don't wanna see him
Watch them drive away

Blindness come come over me
Keep me forever in the dark / No more sun no sun to warm
Warm to unfreeze my heart

Broke the phone into pieces
Don't want to talk to friends / Who want my heart to mend
Watch me turn away

Blindness come come over me
Keep me forever in the dark / No more sun no sun to warm
Warm to unfreeze my heart

Burnt the letters she sent "with love"
Don't want to understand / Or grab a helping hand
Watch me turn bitter

Watch-a-me watch

Blindness come
Come over me
Keep me forever in the dark
No more sun
No sun to warm
Warm to unfreeze my heart

Keep me forever in the dark

Bobby Don't Give No Damn

Bobby does your park bench need fixing
Maybe a painting to hide away the spots
That you have worn away
You don't give a damn anyway

Balding your ego eats away under your hat
The one you stole you won't give it back
Hiding your tears away
You hate having been worn away

The years you spent in the 'stan
And all those desert storms too
You got your commission now you're living
In the morning dew

Your twenty years of service you tucked into your stomach
You belted your tears away in the bar by the wall
Life's perverseness you lost lady luck
You have been eaten away no flowers at your curtain call

You are past intermission rehearsals are of the past
All lines are now action why did you ever last
Past, the first amusement hall
A joke don't you know it
Typecast as the hermit poet

I waved to say hello you stared past me
As if I weren't there at all
I yelled to wake your life's melody
To see if you lived at all

Denying, your ego eats away under your hat
Forgone and forget, you won't take it back
Trying to erase yesterday
You hate having been worn away

Bonny, My Havana Holiday

Bonnie, my Havana holiday
Bonnie, I'll do anything you say
The sun comes out of the lazy sky
Reflects off the water right into my eye

The seagulls turn and fly around
Sometimes landing on the ground
Bonnie my savannah in Havana
Havana holiday

Skin so soft starting to peel
Maybe too much sun
Standing there white and surreal
Maybe have some fun

Sneaking peeks at one another
Looking as if sister and brother
It's a fantasy Havana holiday

We were perfect for one another
We don't understand each other
Helps to keep us guessing
What the other is dressing up or down

Bonnie, my Havana holiday
Bonnie, I'll do anything you say

My hand's around your waist
Let me take us higher
It's not even late
I'm not even tired

But all the while
The sun is going down
It starts to
When it rises from the ground
The sun oh so

Landing into the sea
And now
All that's left
On the beach
Is you and me
Adrift in the richness of what could be
Floating drifing
Abye sea

Bonnie, my Havana holiday
Let's do everything we say

My hand is around your waist
Let me take us higher
It could be late
But we're not even tired

Bonnie I'm glad that I came with you
If I stayed home I'd know not what to do

With you here
And me there
It would have been boring
Now it's you and me asleep was I snoring

Bonnie, my Havana holiday
Skin so soft so peeling so simply appealing
Scintillating don't keep me waiting
Bonnie when we get back
Let's toss out what we lack through it into a sack to get on track
We found a bliss without risk not even hit or miss
A personal nirvana lets go on a lets go on another
Another Havana
Havana holiday

Bourbon Sheets

fell to sleep under bourbon sheets
under dark and stormy skies
wash away some sullen days
of foreboding forbiddens
fell to sleep on black water streets
under evergreen lies
wasted away those yesterdays
when there thundered derision

dark and stormy the leer of beer
streets of bourbon and the fun of fear
it's a fine wine to cross and a cross to bear
when you've fallen so far down
that the farthest you'll fall is so ever ever near

kingdom come will come undone
fallen down a deeper well
footloose a fallen deuce
where is the future hidden
blackened sun unfulfilled fun
how far you've ever fell
under a noose is where you choose
to lead follow or be ridden

dark and stormy the leer of beer
streets of bourbon and the fun of fear
its a fine wine to cross and a cross to bear
when you've fallen so far down
that the farthest you'll fall is so ever ever near

But My Mama

My Mama didn't grow me up
To go to bed with you
She put flowers in my hair
Gave me dresses to wear
Gave me love we both shared
But she didn't grow me up
To go to bed with you
She taught me almost all the bible
We shucked sweet corn while
The TeeVee rerunned Gomer Pyle
But Mama didn't grow me up
To go to bed with you

We can walk holding hands
We can go parking
We can talk folding words
Of how far we've gone tonight
And how long is far but

My Mama didn't grow me up
To go to bed with you
Please keep on your sailor blues
I don't care who paid their dues
This is what I choose to do

Now you can talk your praises
Woo me with fancy phrases
Even wet me with fresh daises
But Mama didn't grow up me
To go to bed with you

Bye Goodbye

Sitting in this station
I've got a ticket in my hand
Waiting for the next fast train
To take me as far away as I can
Scribbling with this failing pen
I try to write you now
Later I'll never find the time
Nor the what the where the how
The time was wrong to say goodbye
Leaving you in that way
The reasons why won't hide the lies
I wish I could only stay

(Chorus:)
Bye Goodbye if I ever stop I'll write
Bye Goodbye it's gonna be a long long night
Bye Goodbye please I'll be alright
Bye Goodbye

I'm going to where this train takes me
Then I'll get off and take another
Why I ever ended it completely
Writing to 'member it's gonna get tougher

(Bridge)
Endless nights without a lover
Sleepwalking days without love
Afternoons endless no something or other

I'm trying to write
To properly say goodbye
But the lights not right
And I think I'm gonna die

(Repeat chorus as you shuffle off to Buffalo)

Casanova

The past lays behind me
Crying out like a gutter drunk
Pleading me to come back
While most of it stunk

I'm sitting wearing my heart on my sleeve
It's spring outside / yet I'm torn apart inside
Been crying so long lost my sensibility
The love I tried / you bled it till it died

Now I'm alone with endless memories
The past tempts me / things I want to see
Others I'd rather place in a bottle out to sea
Empty memories / they hurt me to see

What I thought was love between me and you
You sat and received / all the love that was in me
When you had enough you threw me away like an old shoe
What you did to me / I'd rather not see
Again

But my past tempts me
Making me not forget the years
Empty memories
Of sweet holidays mixed with the tears

I'm alone with these memories
Making me not forget the years
And what you did to me
And how you did me in
Laughter and now the tears

I'm sitting wearing my doubt inside out
It's spring outside / yet I'm torn apart inside
No laughter at all I'm about to climb a wall
The love I tried / you bled it till it died

Can I Keep It Up

Can I keep it up?
You know who you're talking to?
Can I keep it up?
What kind of question is that?
Can I keep it up?
Yes ma'am till my face is blue
Can I keep it up?
You'll never see better unless you spent the night with an acrobat

Can I keep it up?
Hah, can I make you scream?
Can I keep it up?
Show you how to rock and roll?
Can I keep it up?
Karma sutra you ain't never seen
Can I keep it up?
Mission of positions will make you lose control

(Switch it slow and soulful)
And then there's just sometimes when you have to go it real slow
To make the good times last a little longer didn't you know
Do the fifty yard dash it's whambam (snare hits) whambam (snare hits)
oh damn (snare hits) over and done
But taking the time and doing it slow will send you to kingdom...

Can I keep it up?
You know who you're talking to?
Can I keep it up?
What kind of question is that?
Can I keep it up?
Yes ma'am till my face is blue
Can I keep it up?
You never seen better unless you spent the night with an acrobat

Can I keep it up?
How loud can you scream?
Can I keep it up?

How dark can you dream?
Can I keep it up?
Such a wicked theme
Can I keep it up?
You're gonna need them towels when I make you....

Can I keep it up?
You know who you're talking to?
Can I keep it up?
What kind of question is that?
Can I keep it up?
Yes ma'am till my face is blue
Can I keep it up?
If I can't...If I can't...If I can't...

(Vamp) Pretty little woman, now really, what are you thinking, what kind of question is that?

This is Barrence Whitfield you're talking to. I deliver, signed, sealed, as it were. I'm an Agent Provocateur.

Ever on target, Never hit or miss. A tryst is not but a tryst. Supposing if I can't, you know I will drop to my knees.

To do as you please, I won't be a tease, there's no doubt, I will eat...I will eat...I will eat without a doubt, I will eat...
...my hat.

One for Mr. Barrence Whitfield of Barrence Whitfield & The Savages. Legal name, Barry White, but that is another anecdote for another time. At a solo gig, Barrence was trying to interject a ballad into his high-octane performance. With that dip in the trajectory, his friends wanted to know why the ballad? Why take it slow? *Can't you keep it up?* was heard. Innuendos then flew every-which-way. This song formed when I could find a napkin and also a pen at the bar. Another lyrical, finely crafted, and yet tossed to the wayside for not hitting the mark, theirs not mine. Up for grabs for all the Rocking Riddim and Blues singers still in the house. Customized for free, hats and towels on your own dime.

Catch A Fire

(Kantistaro:)
Dorothy wants to catch a fire
Lock it up in a puzzle box
Catch a fire catch a fire
Dorothy wants to catch a fire
Lock it up in a puzzle box
Keep a fire that'll never stop

There's a fire on the patio
Another in the rosebushes
Can you say fire in Esperanto
That's what I want to know
That's all I want to know

(Kantistaro)

My sweetheart needs a spark
Our love has died she's cried
The modern world has a cold cold heart
We need a lotta fire to start
She needs a lotta fire to start

(Kantistaro)

Dorothy has burned the bed
She's even scorched the drapes
It's gone too far I have said
Dorothy just turns her head
Turns to burn down the bed

(Ke kantistaro)

Cathy Said

Cathy said her past was too stale
So she threw hers away in the mail
Cathy said her present was too tense
So she massaged it a little
Cathy said to look into the future
And let the guitars wail (oooo)

Oh my Cathy oh my I'm
Reaching reaching for tomorrow
For Cathy said yesterday was lost
Reaching reaching for tomorrow
Mind no matter what the cost
Now its nighttime in Toronto
And tomorrow is more than just another day

So Cathy oh my I
Reached too far for your tomorrows
And found a Newsweek on your lap
Reaching reaching for the future
And found your lips a bit too chapped
Reached too far for your yesterdays
And found tomorrow is just another day

Cousin Bob Wears Tennis Shoes

(To the tune of that jaunty little tune "Woman From Tokyo" from those heartthrobs, Deep Purple.)

Chartered a ride on TWA / People not caring what you say
This is a whole new edition / I can feel it in my heart
Cousin Bob wears tennis shoes they really clean his feet
Cousin Bob wears tennis shoes makes him look real neat

Cousin Bob swims down a stream / Throwing up on a Dairy Queen
Bob is such an idiot / He's a greaser too
Cousin Bob wears tennis shoes they really clean his feet
Cousin Bob wears tennis shoes they make him look so sweet

But I am here and Bob is there
When push comes to shove
Gets his jacket and leather gloves
He soon will be jamming
In the black of night
And I'm stuck here lips to a pipe

Jamming into the noon / Getting kicks hanging a moon
Bob's such a greaser / I can't get high

Cousin Bob wears tennis shoes they really clean his feet
Cousin Bob wears tennis shoes it makes him look real neat
Cousin Bob wears tennis shoes

During high school, the band that I hung out with and did sound for, grunted PA speakers up flights of stairs for, did not play a whiff of original stuff. Or at least that's how I wanted to remember it. I have since found out they did a few originals, which I, as the sound guy, most certainly knew but conviently forgot for the first edition of this folio. In a blatant attempt to get some words of mine sung, I tried this one out. They already knew the music. Shoo-in. Done deal. But, no deal. The guys just wanted to play gigs and keep the girls as fans in the audience. Funny wasn't in their playbook. At least not this brand of funny if you wanted to hang with the girls afterward. Alas, Cousin Bob never took off. I do admit it was cooler hearing them sing about that woman from Tokyo than anything concerning some idiot named Cousin Bob.

Cross That Line

dress me up in silk and leather
and you'll be more than halfway there
the more expensive the better
cross that line only if you dare

the best in me is the worst in you
definitely worth your while
buy me things very exotic things
cross that line and make me smile

take me where you've never been
secrets too rough to be told
tug at that heart you want to win
cross that line be that bold

pleasure and pain the sweetest refrain
keeps you wondrin' and insecure
perfect sex is my novocaine
but i'm not bluffin' just remember
there's a cross to bear and a line to cross
i can take you to heaven
i can take you to heaven
i can take you to heaven
double-cross me babe and
you can go to hell

waste my time to set me straight
is how the french say au contraire
watch all your things disintegrate
cross that line only if you dare

the best in me is the worst in you
treat me like trash you'll be taken out
screw with me and we're through
cross that line and you'll find out

dress me up in silk and leather

you know where to string the pearls
you can cry you can whisper
cross that line and you own the world

pleasure and pain the sweetest refrain
keeps you wondrin' and insecure
perfect sex is my novocaine
but i'm not bluffin' just remember
there's a cross to bear and a line to cross
i can take you to heaven
i can take you to heaven
i can take you to heaven
double-cross me babe and
you will go to hell

Define femme fatale.

Dangerous Findings

Dangerous findings
Dangerous findings
Dangerous findings
Your dangerous mind is
Taking hold of my life

Making me walk a very fine line
One aimed into the madness time
Your razor sharp with cutting lines
In stories I once held to be fine

Dangerous findings
Dangerous findings
Dangerous findings
Your dangerous mind is
Taking hold of my life

Skittering along the edge of a razor
Bullet talk every third word a tracer
Took a vow to do everything and more
But your love needs to pin at danger

Dangerous findings
Dangerous findings
Dangerous findings
Your dangerous mind is
Taking hold of my life

You want me to dance on the edge
Beat me even-steven then caress
Massage torn intentions and then rest
My weary head against your breast

Skittering along the edge of the razor
Skittering along the edge of the razor
Skittering along the edge of the razor
Skittering along embracing danger

Dear Sir

(Lyrics by Christiane D. Leach & David Greenberg)

Dear Sir, dear sir, very dreary dear sir (x 3)

handshakes sneak on through
leases liens please do
take all you want for you
grease your palms
so ever so calm

lies lay with smiles
smiles all the while
your magic beads
make do do try with these
in exchange for your land
land to seed, bleed, slash and burn detree'd
need, need, see we need to feed, eat, to stay alive
survive
as you bleed the world
dry

cash dollars run to the city
dreams dry dirty & gritty
push aside your wise
bellicose lies
these are no blessings in disguise
leave the rest to rot
empty food pot
land drain waste
till there's nothing left to taste
our eden be on fire

smiles gleam
in exchange for our dreams, scenes, self-esteem
moonbeams
diamond rings, glittery
fluttery wings of false desire,
we know we all know

these lies can never take us higher

Dear Sir, dear sir, sincerely really dear sir
Dear Sir, dear sir, very dreary dear sir

take your contracts
eat them swallow back
double talk backwards walk
your legalese
sound defeating
but
you be forgetting
the melody of our beating hearts
between the words you
thought cleverly blown apart
re-congeal
finally feel
hearts beating to heal
to seal the ill up to no good deal
we gonna sing
we got a song to sing
gonna sing
we gonna sing
we got a song to sing
gonna sing
we gonna sing
we got a song to sing!

hear us sing
unity rings pendulum swings
oh yes, sing our words,
be and live our words
see
they'll make you tremble
your lies lay with lies that be thy trouble
what goes around comes around
gonna take you down
all while
our eden takes us higher

higher than your wings of false desire
today deals with the liars
only lead to
eden on fire
on fire

we gonna sing
we got a song to sing
gonna sing
we gonna sing
we got a song to sing
gonna sing

Jahdub of IR::Indigenous Resistance, who seemingly can be everywhere at
once and still be nowhere in the physical world, and DJ SoySos, of Pittsburgh,
created a track from a Jahdub field recording of Ethiopian drummers. Asian
Dub Foundantion's DrDas added a bassline, then Christiane D. and I set about
creating lyrics about the land grab taking place by corporations, governments,
and the like from just plain common folk whose rights are not upheld. A big task
for sure, and there might be/should be more songs flowing around this theme
from all sides of the equation. This here is the first draft. Once Christiane D.
got in front of the mic and the mood, she free-flowed around this framework of
thoughts and rhymes.

Do We Know Any Allman Bros.?

Do we know any Allman Bros.
That's like asking do we know Dickie Smothers
We don't know them personally
But we know them financially

Albert Caruthers, dear old Dad and Mother
But do we know any Allman Bros.
That's like asking do we know Tommy Smothers
We know how they make their money
Doing a comedy act that's not even funny

Oh yes, we want to be rich and famous
But please,
OH please don't you blame us
For your troubles and woes
Pretty baby we just want to play for you
And take away all your dough

Do we know any Allman Bros.
There's Duane, but he's dead
There's Berry, but he ate a bus
There's Greg, but he's a head
And their primitive songs are full of sex and lust

(Spoken:)
Hmmm, maybe we should get to know them?
Can you humm a few bars, take us up to your room,
professionally speaking, to, ah check out the lyrics?
Tie me to a whipping post, ahhhh yes!

You can hear the parents now
"They're a filthy crowd"
"They play much too loud"

Do we know any Allman Bros.
There's Duane and Berry and Greg
Dead, dead and a head

And everyone's playing them to death
Heard Whipping Post a hundred times no less

So when you ask
Do we know any Allman Bros.
You'd be better served
Asking for Frank Zappa or his Mothers

Another attempt at humor; a sad and adolescent try indeed. Though, to be
honest, I was in my teens then. I most likely thought I was aiming for a Frank
Zappa spin at satire: I missed that target by a mile. It seemed like everyone in
High School was into the Allman Brothers or Led Zeppelin, so, of course, I veered
way outside that circle and still do. I fell in love with *Eat A Peach* after I nabbed a
free album with a subscription to Rolling Stone and then going back through the
Allman Bros catalog track by track, I became a fan, but that was later, after this
lyrical. I guess I'm putting this in here to get those slings and arrows for being
that callous fool, though I would like to state I am not the only one in that club.
Unless no one in the history of high schools has ever filled that niche.

Don't Drink My Beer Buddy Polka

Don't drink my beer buddy
Don't even THINK 'bout it buddy
For every little sip'll give you one fat lip
Buddy don't you drink my beer

Yet another ditty for my spec film script, *Sticks and Stones*. I wrote a scene for the protagonist, Sydney, to take place in one of the dark and dingy Polish bars in the East Village; those almost empty hangouts hardly anyone knew about back then in the early '80s—unhip places with the beer prices hanging as loose as the decorations and about as cheap. I wanted to add a bit of humor and tension to the scene by having an original polka playing in the background. Since I knew the basics, as spec scripts are rarely sold, I wanted to have fun with my imagined "soundtrack" to keep me in a good mood while writing. Around then, while I knew the impossible odds of getting my spec script filmed, I feared the ultimate futility of trying to nab a good agent, or even a lousy agent, with one. Which, by the by, turned out to be true. No agent. No film. Hollywood was just a sign, not a destination, for me. At least I got my laughs in when I could.

Drip Dry

Rainy rainy rainy day
Time to cough my thoughts away
Rainy rainy rainy day
And who am I to really say

The Jackman plays with his jacks
The ball'n'chain he must put back
The fire hydrant starts to scream
The Jackman lives in his dirty dreams

Rainy rainy rainy day
Must remember to put my books away
Rainy rainy rainy day
Do you think I could really stay

The trainman's lantern's lost
The conductor his boss
Is getting on my nerves
I'll see he gets just what he deserves

I'll have them go and take his mother away
I'll have him know
That she'll have to go

She can be repossessed
Just like all the rest
They'll have to take his mother away
I'll see what he has to say

But who is he to really say
That we can't put the old lady away
Or if it's really not a rainy day
It could be some other train going by
With no steam to gather up a sigh

Rainy rainy rainy day
Time to put my thoughts away

Rainy rainy rainy day
Leaving my thoughts in dissarray

To play fancy with my ideas
Commit myself to overseers
And the lantern's lost the train can't go on it's way
The fog is trying to lift and leave today

The trainman gets his lantern he goes his way
Can you stand to understand why

Nursery school children read from books
And give us all very funny looks
Someday they will have to learn
That all their books they will have to burn

Rainy rainy rainy day
I have thrown all my thoughts away
Rainy rainy rainy day
And to live each day as today

Dropping

Comes a time for sweaters
Comes a time for coats
Under there you can hide laughter
Under there you got room to gloat

Turning little colder can't you feel
Turning little colder can't you see
All the icy shoulders and the fallen leaves

Some try to call it The FALL
Others laugh and call it DECLINE
It's too cold to tell jokes at all
Besides none are better'n mine

Turning little colder can't you feel
Turning little colder can't you see
All the icy shoulders and the fallen leaves

Temperatures dropping can't you feel
Temperatures dropping can't you tell
Lovers are walking in empty shells

Electric Appliance Day

It's an electric appliance day
Can't be any other way
All day long all night too
It can't be all that wrong

Sing to the stove yell to the freezer
In the alcove sitting there
Freezing away
All night and all day

Pay homage to the clock
It won't work when it's in hock
Pray down to the Westinghouse
No chill refrigerator
It won't work but it'll arouse

It's an electric appliance day
It can't be any other way
All day long all night too
It can't be all that wrong

We are marching
We are marching
To the kitchen
To the kitchen
To the alcove
To pay homage
To the...coffee grinder (grind me silly)

We are walking we are sitting
In the ice cream type parlor chairs

Sitting pay homage to the electric appliances
All the carnage of the electric appliances

Plug yourself in feel the current
Plug yourself in feel it surge

One hundred twenty volts or so
Lots of watts into you
Plug yourself in are you breathing
Plug yourself in stop the wheezing

All the stuff in the kitchen
Have to do it every day

Relaxing with electricity
Gets him to work all day
It pleasures him that he shows it
By plugging you in
By plugging you into
One hundred and twenty volts

It's an electric appliance day
It can't be any other way
All day long all night too
It can't be all that wrong
It's very fun to do

Plug yourself in
Plug yourself in
Plug yourself in
A very fast trip...to heaven (you wish)

Pay homage to your friends
They will speak to you
Talk to them slowly
They will respond to you
Then you'll know what to do

Endings

alone left with traces of you left in the places where you stole my heart
bittersweet treats of summer heat young lovers undercover in the dark
fingertips letting slip how you felt for me holding me so
you held the hand that held my soul sweet-goddamn when did you
know

we talked of our deepest hurts we threw our darkest thoughts into the
fire
when did you know we were through when did you find us lost when did
the end start
you kissed me a thousand times we counted them all damnitall was it
then
our endless summer fell into fall hitting a wall and over and over asking
when

when?

when did the end start
when did the lies begin
were you telling me how much you loved me whispering it'd be forever
was it then
when did your heart break
i need to know the ending
keeping me in the dark like it was all a lark looking for another
another "friend"

when?

when did the end start
when did the lies begin
were you telling me how much you loved me whispering it'd be forever
was it then
when did your heart break
i need to know the ending
keeping me in the dark like it was all a lark looking for another
another way to end
it all?

before you froze me out your kisses held little doubt i'd be forever in
your heart
secrets we shared with dreams with dreams we owned it all always
laughing at disaster
you were my everything and now night never ends midnight and the
hours after
i wonder who you're kissing now and where he's kissing you when did
the end start

fingertips letting slip how I felt about you
secrets held now letting go but need to know
when did the end start

Everything (love song nr. 85)

In a fit of inspiration
I'll write to you
With a bit of perspiration
I'll run to you
You mean everything to me
I mean that I do

Under great determination
I try to sleep
Under those puffs of elation
You've given me
You mean everything to me
I mean that I do

You mean everything
Meaning without you
I cease to be
Everything (Anything)

In the late of evening
I'll turn to you
With kisses soothing
Melting into you
You mean everything to me
I mean that I do

With a bit of inspiration
I'll write to you
In a fit of determination
I'll run to you
You mean everything to me
I mean that I do

Evolution

Got your Daddy's arms and legs
Got your Mommy's face
Got your Daddy's sense of humor
And suburban taste

(Chorus:)
Give it back give it all back back back
This is no tag sale
You've got to you've got to make yourself
You can't buy it wholesale
Give it back give it all back back back
Stand on your own two legs
Climb up a peg give it all back

Got your sisters boyfriend
Got his deodorant
Got to wash his socks
Got to wear his pants

Got your girlfriends and their chit chat
Got dumb remarks got bitter pacts
Got loaded questions got no targets
Even got a subscription to TRUE LOVE comix

You got a sense of bizness
You got common sense
Always your good life
Is over the fence

(Chorus)

Got your Daddy's state of mind
So bright you blind us
You got his nose for values
Got your Mother's sinus

Got your Daddy's healthy hair

(Give it back give it all back)
Got your Mother's looks
(Give it back give it all back)
Got her eye for fashion
(Give it back give it all back)
Got a library book
(Give it back give it all back)
Got a woman's intuition
(Give it back give it all back)
Got a woman's sex
(Give it back give it all back)
Got a man's sense of danger
(Give it back give it all back)
Got Dad's doggy fixed
(Give it back give it all back)
Got a good set of legs
(Give it back give it all back)
Got a set of dangerous curves
(Give it back give it all back)
Got all of my loving
(Give it back give it all back)
Got all of my aching heart
(Give it back give it all back)
Got every single one of my thoughts so I can't think straight I don't even
know my name baby 'cos you even got that on the tip of your tongue
(Give it back give it all back)

(Reminder: Anything in a set of these parentheses denotes a back-
ground chorus except where it instructs the uninitiated to the wherefore
of the lyricals bits of the chorus and where to insert the chorus back into
the song between a verse. Or for these kind of notes on how to figure it
all out, but that you might want to do without and get right on repeating
the chorus, or perhaps noting where the background chorus should be
singing that sweet old repeating line of the lyricals above. Got dat? If so,
give it back.)

Faery

The façade of the building
Crept toward the sky
As the bundler went faggotting
As if the world would die

The phantasm of the child
Was to soar like a fly
The wish itself was very mild
And the child very shy

He sold his sticks too low
Paying off his knickers,
(Over his knees) where his cut shows
Flesh caught on prickers.

As he ran through field and wood,
Through feuds of service
A hollow determined to unhood
The boy's direct purpose

The valley served it's homily
And the boy knelt on moss
His own fight to live fought to flee
And another life was lost

If he was meant to live this wouldn't happen
Where a youngster of five his whole insides
Rot out before he's six and he's left to die
In the feud of the valley under a pelisse of moss

In my mind, I have always heard bassist John Wetton as the vocalist on this one.
Perhaps, in my mind, I'm too much of a King Crimson serflet?

Farewell

The snow falls into my eyes
Making it hard for me to see
The clouds surround the ground
While the snow flies about me

People coming, people going, people not knowing
Flying, smiling, yelling, screaming, people not knowing

People smiling, people crying, people not caring
Flying, going, yelling, screaming, people not caring

The snow falls on cars
Of people who meant a lot to me
My fears cloud my eyes
Making it hard for me to see

People caring, people going, people not knowing
Flying, smiling, yelling, screaming, people not knowing

The snow falls into my eyes
Making it hard for me to see
The clouds surround the ground
While the snow flies about me

Trying to set me free
Trying for heaven's sake
To believe in farewell

Feets Move

Hey feets gotta dance that beat
Feets gotta cross that street
Feets move 'cos it's that neat
Feets gotta stamp those feets

Ya gotta Mersey beat
Ya gotta Copper beat
Ya gotta Nick who's beat
Ya can't go home to sleep
Ya gotta stamp your feet

Tell me the latest news
When your dreams come true
Tap out the latest tunes
Wear out your bestest shoes

Hey feets gotta dance that beat
Feets gotta cross that street
Feets move cos it's that neat
Feets gotta stamp those feets

Ya gotta percale sheets
Ya gotta dead end streets
Ya gotta destitution
Ya gotta constipation
Ya gotta radio playing

Linda calls it a disgrace
We'll just have to stomp her face
And leave not one trace
We'll have an empty space

Where feets can dance that beat
Feets gotta cross that street
Feets move cos it's that neat
Feets gotta stamp those feets

Ya gotta Mersey beat ya gotta reggae beat ya gotta classic beat
Ya gotta English Beat ya gotta 'Merican beat ya gotta Cuban beat
Ya gotta atomic bombs ya gotta gollywogs ya gotta discrimination
Ya gotta change the nation ya gotta lots of dead ya gotta pipes of lead

Ya gotta get got gone giggle

Written in the days and under the haze of Elvis Costello's *Armed Forces* with
such songs as "Goon Squad," "Two Little Hitlers," and the like. These days, one
can't be having thoughts about erasing Linda, the not-so-innocent bystander,
from the above imagined scene, can we? Nope, not even in a song trying to de-
fang those goons of the far-right-wangers. A little bit of Ludovico reprogramming
upon the lyricist will be needed to ready these lyrics for their airing out in public.

Floating

Go tripping the light fantastic and
Fall flat on your face
Talk double talk with preening
Your words have no taste
Everyone will gladly listen
And they won't understand
Your love will be floating
But no one no no one will wanna
Hold your hand

You'll float away
You'll float away
Floating away
Floating away alone

Lead me down the road to Babel and on
Promise me where it's at
I'll follow careening
Between ruts on the beaten paths
All my songs forgotten
Feet stuck in quicksand
Tulalularay gone floating
No one no one no no one will wanna
Hold my hand

(Bridge:)
Just want to strip it all away / Take it down to bare facts
Keep it simple keep it clean / Wash away wash away wash away
Dry it all on brass tacks / And float astray on the noon rays of the lazy
hazy days of wonder

You'll float away
You'll float away
Floating away
Floating away alone

Lead me down the road to Babel and on

Promise me where it's at
Won't follow careening
On downtrodden beaten paths
All I've said you've forgotten
No matter where I stand
Goodbye go floating
Not one no one no no one will wanna
Hold your hand

Go float away
Go float away
Floating away
Away away
Tulalularay
Alone

Ford Gone So Mad

(Lyrics by Kim Ware & David Greenberg)

Ford gone so mad it's just insane
Got your sixpack, gun rack, glasspack too
Don't look past this look of ultra disdain
Your bumper's hanging on by stickers and glue

Ford gone so mad who woulda thunk it
Half Hazzard paint job but you don't mind
Paid 'em with booze and he done drunk it
Now ya got weird art on your behind

(Chorus:)
Ford gone mad so like a rabid dog
Ford gone so mad a drooling drunk
Ford gone so mad stanking so shitty
Ford gone so mad damn gross road hog
Ford gone so mad stink stank stunk
Ford gone so mad like F for Flunk One Fifty
Ford gone
So mad

(Bridge:)
Ford's gone so mad and Chevys and Dodges even seen
      Toyotas so fucked so bad
Vdubs and Kias rotten to the core with gaffer tape and cellophane
      for windows and doors
Temper tantrums destroyed fuselages not one iota of smarts
      so sad
Fails of paint fails of decorum and decor hitting rock bottom
      the caveman's floor
Ford gone
So mad

Ford gone so mad a sad refrain
Got your stogies, hoagies, fresh leaf too
Rolling coal on the libtards oh so inane
Bumper stickers everywhere yes up the wazoo

Ford gone so mad who woulda thunk it
Half Hazzard paint job but you don't mind
Paid 'em with booze and he done drunk it
The 1980s have left your sorry ass far behind

(Chorus:)
Ford gone mad so like a rabid dog
Ford gone so mad a drooling drunk
Ford gone so mad stanking so shitty
Ford gone so mad damn gross road hog
Ford gone so mad stink stank stunk
Ford gone so mad like F for Flunk One Fifty
Ford gone
So mad

Galdino Pataxo Warrior

(Music by Sawandi Simon / Lyrics by David Greenberg and Jah9 /
Spoken word by The Ghost & Zumbi)

(The Ghost, Spoken:) When I was at the trial of Galdino's murderers in
Brasilia, one of the moments permanently etched in my memory was
when I was meeting Galdino's family and one of the Pataxo warriors
handed to me the coroners photo of Galdino. It showed his burnt body
90 percent of which was covered with third degree burns, the result of
him being set on fire as a joke. It was a sight absolutely horrifying.

The poor die forgotten swept under the rug
For the rich and the famous gossip is their nightly drug
News is news when everyone knows your name
But who is really to blame

Indigenous resistance to the media hype
Truth is what they need so it isn't what they like
Indigenous resistance to the status quo
Truth is what you need
Now its time you know
Now its time you know

───────────

Released on *IR24 Galdino 2010 EP, IR24.2 Galdino Mixes* & *IR25 Dubversive* on
the IR::Indigenous Resistance label. Check us out at dubreality.com, dubreality.
wordpress.com, dubreality.bandcamp.com and as Indigenous Resistance on
all your favorite streaming services and, please, not from some torrent or a free
download URL. Especially those ending in dot-r-u!

Go For Broke

(Intro section:)
Easier to break than to build
Breakdown what little love's left
Breakdown what you will

What was yours I want to be mine
Treat me well and I'll be fine
I'll still say what's on my mind
Gonna break you in two this time

Can't stop feeling this way
Can't stop when I go for broke

Love me with what little love's left
Sing sweet nothings I'm tone deaf
Buddy boy oh pal o' mine
Gonna break you in two this time

Can't stop feeling this way
Can't stop when I go for broke

Hold onto what you've got left
Soon enough you'll be bereft
Without even one skinny little dime
Gonna break you in two this time

Can't stop feeling this way
Can't stop when I go for broke

(Bridge:)
A broken heart you can't fix if your love light's dark
A broken toy you can't fix with a bundle of joy
A broken home you can't fix if you're home alone
A broken man
A broken man
A broken man you understand
Can't still stand on his own two feet

When you're down and out and broke
I'll confuse you with the smoke
Of burning lies and tasteless jokes
Can't stop you still have some hope

Can't stop feeling this way
Can't stop when I go for broke

Run scared run wild run free
I can still make you bend at the knees
Here's the ladder here's the rope
Can't stop you still have some hope

Can't stop feeling this way
Can't stop when I go for broke

(C&W version of the bridge. While you're at it, add a few fiddles to the mix and those heavenly Nashville background singers who hang on every sigh and then get this sucker on to the youngster vying to be the next Waylon or Willie; in other words, the next of the rough and tumble Outlaw Countrymen and not the clean-cut crew of contemporary Nashville dudes doing the old push and shove to reach top ten popdom before all others.)

A broken life ya can't fix by buying a wife
A broken lamp ya can't fix if your feet are damp
A broken chair ya can't fix when your're not there
A broken bone ya can't fix over the telephone
A broken man
A broken man
A broken man ya understand
Can't stand with an empty glass in his hand

Get Back In The Backseat

mashing in the backseat get your legs outta my face
mashing in the backseat no no not yet not yet
mashing in the backseat that's success you taste
mashing in the backseat don't take the suckers bet
mashing in the backseat

get back get back get back to where you once belonged
get back in the backseat

mashing in the backseat gimme gimme some of your face
mashing in the backseat show me how tough you can get
mashing in the backseat don't leave a minute to waste
mashing in the backseat don't make the photo finish yet
mashing in the backseat

get back get back get back to where you once belonged
get back get back better get your ass back
back in the backseat

Ah youth: wild, untamed, youth. Or at least the fevered comic book version of
"wild, untamed, youth" before the Comics Code Authority slapped them down
and cleaned them up in the 1950s. This one is for the ladies, as Joan Jett was the
imagined protagonist singing into the rearview mirror when I pencilled this one
in one of my notebooks. And yes, I do know of her sexual preferences.

Going Back

Going back to the autumn before last winter
Always before and always never and never even later

The road lies in it's beaten autumnal splendor
The dreamer tries to begin again always wants his more

The dead and sorry leaves lay tired
On the cold and wet tar
The dreamer with his suitcase
Thinks that home is not so far

Was it then or was it now trying to remember
Always before and always never and never even later

Scrapbook pictures of ladybugs and sledding in December
Ignoring jokes against me and of ethnic character

In the cellar
The spider webs perform
Against a carpet of black
And of dreams deformed
Of always coming back

Going back
I'm going home
Going back
I'm going home
Going back
I'm dilly dallying

Going back
It's thought rallying—going back, going, I'm coming home

Phrase after phrase of talk trying to remember
Always before and always never and never even later

Breaking wires of suspension of the poisoning spider

They barricade a net before the family picture

As if to leave me out
Of the family funk
They impede my passage
Moving my movements seemingly drunk

I'm going back
I'm going home

To scrapbook days
Of Ektachrome® memories
Old people I never knew
And a me I still can't believe

I'm going back
I'm going home
I'm going back
I'm dilly dallying

My memory seems clouded
As if to say I was never there
Pictures conjure up names
Of people who might've cared

Going back to the autumn before the winter
Always before and always never and never even later

The road lies in its beaten autumnal splendor
The dreamer tries to begin again always wants his more

The dead and sorry leaves
On the cold and wet tar
The dreamer with his suitcase
Thinks that HOME is not so far

Gone

(Music by Grace Kelly / Lyrics by Grace Kelly & David Greenberg)

Where did you go? / Why have you gone?
Have you forgotten that I was the only one / The times we had
The love we shared / You made it so real
I thought you really cared

Gone gone gone away gone gone away going on
I was there always there and you walked
Walked away from the love that we shared [x2]

When you're not here / Half of me's gone
Confused and alone no end to the day / No place to belong

When did you know / You'd be moving on?
Your embrace said it all at least in my mind / So so blind

Gone gone gone away gone gone away going on
I was there always there and you walked
Walked away from the love that we shared [x2]

When you're not here / Half of me's gone
Confused and alone no end to the day / No place to belong

When did you know / You'd be moving on?
Your embrace said it all at least in my mind / So so blind
Where did you go? / Why have you gone?

Grace Kelly, the musician, was working on this her bossa-nova break-up song
and wanted some tweaking, all before she went into the studio. Within a few
days. No pressure, none, at all. With a bit of back and forth, on Facebook no less,
here it is. "Gone" is on her 2011 album, *The Man With The Hat*, a collaboration
with Phil Woods & Monty Alexander. To me, it sounds like an end-of-summer
song, the oh-so-blue-tinged longing over the summer romance you hoped would
last forever, when the days get cooler, the nights get longer, and the reality of
school begins. Not that I had any experience with any of those torn-to-shreds
endings of summer, sadly, and yet, in hindsight, happily.

Grind Them 'Till You Find Them

Get in control get your hands on the wheel
Grab it at three and nine oh yeah
Don't be scared ease into the feel
Slam it and you'll be fine oh yesssssssss

Grind 'em
Grind 'em 'til you find 'em
Grind 'em
Grind 'em 'til you find 'em
Grind 'em
Grind 'em 'til you find 'em
Four on the floor the breeze in your hair
Show me more show me more show me more if you dare

Grind 'em
Grind 'em 'til you find 'em
Grind 'em
Grind 'em 'til you find 'em
Grind 'em
Grind 'em 'til you find 'em
When you're in gear don't hesitate
Take it slow take it slow take it slow but don't ever break

(bridge:)
Unless you
Clutch it
Clutch it
Clutch it
Get it into gear baby
Clutch it
Clutch it
Clutch it
Get it, get it, get it, get it into gear baby

Take your time you know what I like
Ease into those curves oh babe
When you turn left you make it right

I'm at a loss for words oh yesssssssss

Grind 'em
Grind 'em 'til you find 'em
Grind 'em
Grind 'em 'til you find 'em
Grind 'em
Grind 'em 'til you find 'em
Four on the floor the breeze in your hair
Show me more show me more show me if you dare

Grind 'em
Grind 'em 'til you find 'em
Grind 'em
Grind 'em 'til you find 'em
Grind 'em
Grind 'em 'til you find 'em
When you're in gear don't hesitate
Take it slow take it slow but don't ever break

(Blues break)
Don't ever break
Don't ever break
Don't ever slam on the breaks little baby darling girl when you've been
driving so damn fine
Unless you caress that clutch like it was a rare bottle of wine at the end
of time
If you don't then just

Grind 'em
Grind 'em 'til you find 'em
Grind 'em
Grind 'em 'til you find 'em
Grind 'em
Grind 'em 'til you find 'em
(Yeah repeat and fuck up that clutch all through the fade out)

Innuendo much? This one is craving to transmutate into a full-blown-ass blues.

Hands Down

Giving me words you've heard in conversation
I don't I don't want to hear it
Giving me words you've heard on television
I don't I don't want to hear it
Sit down let me make you understand
Lay back you can talk talk with your hands

You flip thru flip thru flip thru magazines
I don't I don't want to hear it
You know the who, what, where, and why of every scene
I don't I don't want to hear it
Sit down let me make you understand
Lay back you can talk talk with your hands

Listen: (Musical break for the clapping of hands in rhythm)
I don't I don't want to hear it
(Repeated as a chorus and broken up into polyrhythms befitting King
Sunny Adé, Fela Kuti, Kanda Bongo Man or Akon's dad, the regal king of
percussion, Mor Thiam)

Conversing everything I don't need to hear
I don't I don't want to hear it
You do talk talk as if it's silence that you fear
I don't I don't want to hear it
Sit down let me make you understand
Lay back you can talk talk with your hands

Giving me words you've heard in conversation
I don't I don't want to hear it
Giving me words you've heard on television
I don't I don't want to hear it
Sit down let me make you understand
Lay back you can talk talk with your hands
Sit down (lay back) you can talk talk with your hands

Heaven Can Wait

I give you caviar you give me smelt
I give you kisses you never even felt
I give you flowers you'd rather sneeze
I'm dying here you said would you
Please

I made furious love you called it a nap
I could take you there but you burnt the map
Cupid aimed his arrow, you shot him in the back
I have a heart of gold, it's the sanity that I
Lack

Up is down, and love, love is hate
One night with you is like forever and a day
I'm falling down a bottomless well
Heaven can wait if it's going to be hell
Heaven can wait if it's going to be hell
Heaven can wait if it's going to be hell

(Repeat and take two ibuprofen and call me in the morning of the day
when the royalty check is in the mail.)

Oh, those surf-rocking Russians, the Red Elvises! At Rykodisc, after being
bought out by Mr. Chris Blackwell, producer of Bob Marley and, at that point, ex-
owner of Island Records, we merged for a bit with his newly incorporated Palm
Pictures outfit. Not quite a year later, he dissolved our Salem offices and moved
almost everyone to New York City. Before those unnerving times, and while
still churning out the "hits" for Rykodisc in beautiful downtown Salem, Massa-
chusetts, I was charged to manage the soundtrack album release for the Palm
Pictures film Six String Samurai. Ryko's A&R knew I had that kind of cheeze and
whacked-out humor that the Red Elvises personified, still in my blood from my
Rubber Rodeo video days of the early '80s. I hit it off instantly with the band, of
course, and after attending one spirited concert at SxSW, I had to write these
few lines for Vladimir and the boys. Alas, even the Elvii denied my lyric its day.
However, I often wondered if this could be just the thing for Gogo Bordello. Do
they return my calls? My emails? My lyric-wrapped missiles of bricks thrown
through their hotel windows? Well, those they returned.

He's A Bitch

The night collapses in reverence
Can it be you don't wear the pants
The admirers pray in front of his throne
Their tones chill your bones
Then he leaves you sobbing alone

He controls you
He has his hold of you
No matter what you try
He still knows he has spies

He's a man
Who holds the keys in his hands
He's a man
Who knows he's a man in command
He's the man
Who takes your hand out of his hand
Oh he's a man

You lie in bondage held by a few cords
He hovers over you like some war lord
Chinese servant happily hobbling towards the door
Hello master rag wrapped feet that are sore

He's the man
Who eats his heart out literally
He's a man
Who won't take no kiddingly
He wants his now
And he won't take a woman's share
He lives his life
On the edge in the now laid bare

You're the past now brittle
Clear glass icicle
He freezes you out till you melt down
And he won't give it up until you pound

On the door that's now frozen
All he will do is thumb his nose and
Twiddle his thumbs as he lays
Enjoying his fun

He's a man
Holds the keys in his heart of hearts
He's a man
Oh he's a man
Who won't stop ribbing you or let you forget
That he's a man, a man, a man oh man oh man

He's a man
Who locks the door on your hand
Trying to get in he calls you woman!
Yet he's a man
Enjoying the fun while twiddling thumbs
He freezes up before you can melt him down
And he won't give it up until you pound
On emotions half frozen
All he will do is tickle your toes and
Hide his eyes from your poison
While he lays enjoying the toys and
Being a man

He's a man
He's a bitch

Here2There

I'm going from here2there (additup)
It's taking all my time
Always standing on line (I'm)

4ever talking of now and then
Yet dreaming 4 a future
4give me but I make amends
To my sosh thought tutor (as)

Her thoughts are always arriving
While I'll still be striving to grow from here there

(Hook:)
I'm here
I wanna go there
I'm here
I wanna go there
I'm here
Getting me from here2there (additup)

A. is living up to her letters
Even when they're "Return to Sender"
Ever so consciously awake
That she's moving from here2there (and)

I'm going from here2there
But all my friends build walls
Cement of fine mixed lies
And I'm not that clever or tall (I'm)

4ever talking of now and then
And give out little "X"s
Police think I think I'm Jesus
But it's only love and kisses (for)

At times I'm living on love
Though I find it a contradiction
As I'm almost dying

And my words counter di-di-diction (but)

That may be the true good thing
So I don't have to talk while working
To go from here2there (additup)

(Hook:)
I'm here
I wanna go there
I'm here
I wanna go there
I'm here
Getting me from here2there (additup)

(Continue on with that hook here like it won't end and when the groove is finally so infectious...end. Quick.)

Hey Hey New Jersey (Greetings From Ozone Park)

Hey Hey New Jersey
They call you the Garden State
Hey Hey New Jersey
It seems that the nation's late
In seeing what you cultivate

They've found they're ready and born to run
On Bruce's suicide machines
And on Patty Smith's Horses unwon
And her Gloria dreams
They listen to Southside Johnny on the radio

And the runners at the bars seem so alive
Yet dancing so tense
Prancing and shaking like knives in the hands
Of the inexperienced
Listening to the radio of Jersey on the radio
Listening to the radio of Jersey on the radio

Hey Hey New Jersey
They call you the Garden State
Hey Hey New Jersey
It seems that the nation's late
In seeing what you cultivate

For rock & roll the jester's seek the shores
Of Southern Jersey
And quick hip trick kids steal for more
Not trying to be lazy
They listen to Southside Johnny on the radio
Hip tricking the games of life with all
Their suicide friends
Playing romance like the chrome pinball
Of the young Americans
Listening to the radio of Jersey on the radio
Turn it up—turn up—the radio
Turn it up—driving down Jersey with the radio on—go—go

(Driving down Jersey music, don't forget to add in some Jersy Shore
Surf riffs)

Hey Hey New Jersey
They call you the Garden State
Hey Hey New Jersey
It seems that the nation's late
In seeing what you cultivate

Parking beneath the halos of the tanks of Esso Gas
Jester loving in the dark
And the d.j. announces at last "Greetings from Ozone Park"
And we listen to Southside Johnny on the radio

Turn it up—turn up—the radio
Turn it up—driving down Jersey with the radio on—go—go

In This Place

there's a place holds no shadows light sweeping clear to the crackling
        corners
there's a place where love drains away no words just humming on the
        lips of mourners

places places places
answers hidden
certainty falls
the storm rages outside the whipping rain

sadness when placed here in this room turns into dried up husks of
        eternal hours
saw you run behind emotionless curtains bloodless you fell paler than
        graveyard flowers

places places places
answers hidden
certainty falls
the storm rages around your inner mounting flame

this is the place where
this is the place where
this is the place where nothing begins and nothing ends
and nothing from nothing is what you place
in this place in place of your heart

places places places
questions arise
the bonfire falls
ashes dull over your mounting pain

this is the place where
this is the place where
this is the place where nothing begins and nothing ends
and nothing from nothing is what you place
in this place in place of your heart

I'm Not Talking

I'm not talking
That's all I gotta say
You really think you're cool
Man was I really such a fool
To treat me like you do to be used as a tool
With these tales you told in school
That's one thing I can do without

You can say love is lazy
I think you're really crazy
When you say you want it
Then you say "well maybe"
Don't call me baby I'll call you

I'm not talking
That's what I've gotta say
You took me for a fool
To treat me like you do
Now you're cold and cruel
When giving me the screw
That's one thing I can do without

A "restoration" of the mumbled Yardbirds hit. During a few summers of my college years, I was the sound-dude for friends who formed Thunderhill, a very loud and raucous cover band playing bars around Fairfield County. That year's drummer wanted to do a wham-bam version of this tune. Since no one could decipher the lyrics from the record, he asked me to scribble out something for approximating real words to sing. Happening pre-internet and Googling, I guess he was just too cheap to buy the sheet music: saving the money for beers and gas and smokes and such. I jotted down this version during that rehearsal. I was psyched. No band in their right mind would do "Cousin Bob" due to an adherence to their macho rock and roll cred, but this was an homage, an automatic, a, yes, shoo-in! From that night on, the drummer proceeded to mumble his way through the lyrics with every performance. I could have just copied the transliteration of my bar mitzvah passage. No one would have been the wiser. Even Rabbi Silver.

I'm The Baby You're Having

Hey   Hello
Hey   Hello
Hey   Hello

Can you hear me?

I'm
I'm the baby you're having
Yes I'm
I'm the baby you're having

Hey   Hello
Hey   Hello
Hey   Hello

Can you feel me?

Hey
She's having me her baby
Hey
She's saying uh-uh-oh give it to me
Hey
I'm her kid just don't forget
Hey
You haven't given her her rights yet
Hey—don't make her suffer just yet
She's turned into a...ah...ah...suffragette

Another lyrical for Thunderhill, though not that they asked. I wrote it as an answer song to the Paul Anka hit single, "(You're) Having My Baby." Anka wrote the music and words as well, in case you want to throw some shade at those initial lyrics. The first time I heard that song on the radio, I was hit upside the head. How insipidly dumb! After the thousandth play, I couldn't stand it anymore. I was ready to take it to the next logical, comically dumber, step. I knew this would be a great lead-in song for the band to segue into their killer cover version of Bowie's "Suffragette City." Bowie stayed in the repertoire. This one? Still very much unsung. For that, the world is probably a better place.

Is It Hot In Here (Or Is It Just Me?)

(Lyrics by David Greenberg / Music by Mick Leonard)

i have a fever and I don't know his name
dude's burning me up with desire, again
torching my soul with his vicious flame
and then flushing my ashes, down the drain

is it hot in here?
is it hot in here?
is it hot in here?
or is it just me?

i have a fever no i can't be saved
when that guy's around can't help but, misbehave
scorching and burning like a microwave
get busy with me? he would rather, dig my grave

is it hot in here?
is it hot in here?
is it hot in here?
or is it just me?

everywoman's dream with a wicked twist
dances so slow and low i need an, exorcist
in the pocket on the money i can't resist
gangsta with a swagger he doesn't know, i exist

is it hot in here?
is it hot in here?
is it hot in here?
or is it just me?

[Middle break]

he's steaming when he shakes rattles and rolls
when he bites his lip whoa oh oh oh just makes me flip
break the bank what he's got on sale you know i'm sold
want to crush his lips ignite his hips gonna sink his battleship

is it hot in here?
is it hot in here?
is it hot in here?
or is it just me? (x 2)

_____

I wrote this one for my friend Barrence Whitfield, whom I kind of introduced to you pages earlier. If you ever saw Mr. Whitfield back in the day, which would have been sometime in the '80s and somewhere near Boston and with his Savages, this guy was on fire. A bonfire. And he still is, having gotten back with his Savages and kicking over the petrol can every time he steps up to the microphone.

While driving into my job in Brighton one day, (Massachusetts, not the UK), I could picture Barrence on stage beckoning/taunting/beseeching the audience with the chorus in true rock 'n' roller, bomp 'n' roller, jump blues fashion. I hung that chorus around a lyric about a girl who could care less. Guys and Gals, you know the type, and perhaps, sometimes, when the wrong person comes flirting along, you become one of those? Just asking.

Then, all of a sudden, I thought of someone like China Moses, whose "Ridin' The Bad News" is a collab with yours truly (in the R section of this here Mud Folio), or one of my intern alums (the gal singers of course) out there in music land singing their hearts out, under-appreciated. At the same time, Sawandi (from IR) and I were working on a song for the Jamaican dancehall/reggae singer, Keida, unsolicited. Which, as you know by now, unsolicited is shorthand for "when hell freezes over." While female singers were lighting up my neurons anyway, I started rejigging and then flipping lyrics around to the other side of the coin.

Though gals, if you do swing with the gals, then it might be fun to sing it about a girl...which could be a big hit. Perhaps for those who "Kissed A Girl," Jill & Katie, and then there's Cyndi's "When You Were Mine," Lady Gaga's "Poker Face," and on and on. If you want that one, lemme know and I'll keep flipping it to get this one on the right side of your coin.

So there it is, more information than you will ever need behind the piece of fluff that is "Is It Hot In Here [Or Is Just It Me?]" At least la version pour une femme, so to speak. Music was written to this by Mick Leonard for the dude version of this. It might be Savaged up by Mr. Whitfield. It may not. Maybe not as the years have passed, and sadly, so has Mick. Mick, way too soon, way too soon. His demo is so damn good you have to hear it. Email me, babe.

I've Got Plenty (Of Nothing)

You talk you smile all the while
Laughing inside of you laughing at me
Thinking how funny that you've got the money
Enough to buy friends but not me

Why don't I follow your line Pied Piper
Why don't I follow your line sweet talker

You talk you smile all the while
Laughing inside of me laughing at you
Thinking how funny that you've got the money
But you can't own real friends whatever you do

You can't tell me who I am no way
I am who I want to be you don't own me

And don't you tell me who qualifies
As a friend
Don't try to mold me that way
I won't bend
Just because you rate your friends
Like a bottle of wine
Don't you tell me how to
Classify mine

You sit and think my attitude stinks
You just haven't found out who the joke's on
When you finally wake up I'll be gone
Pied Piper

Don't you try to tell me who qualifies
As a friend
Don't try to mold me that way
I won't bend

It's Only How You Said (Compensation)

You must try to understand
The emptiness of my eyes
Why when you stand there
I only start to cry

Please help me
I've lost my cane
I cannot walk my knee
My leg hurts with pain

I'm the actor who strains his neck
Trying to shave
Stock still at my mirror staring
My razor barely behaves

So take out a bayonette and cut out my throat
So I don't have to talk
So sit me in a wheel chair push me around
So I don't have to walk

Is it right for me to dissolve away
That's what the forms say
That's what you say standing there
Coming from you it's not so clear

Please help me
I've lost my cane
I cannot walk my knee
My leg hurts with pain

Burning dust seas
Of limbs aflame
Deserted left to bleed
Legs melt from pain

You must try to understand
The emptiness of my eyes

Why when you stand there
I only start to cry

You must try to understand
The emptiness of my eyes
Why when you stand there
And can only sigh

Jump

Playing with stubs of used cigarettes
Maybe you're nervous
Pushing ashes into your fingernails
You ring for room service
Silent you're bored or depressed
A conversationalist
Staring into the phone short answers
Compiling lists

Smoke that cigarette one last time
Then turn yourself to stone
See the sun trying to shine
Trying to change you from being alone

Change you from alone
Turn you into a person who isn't as loud
As the dumbwaiter's voice over the phone
Or the mission of the people
Under your balcony oblivious
To your frantic solution to your trouble

Jump you say so what's the delay
Instead of the rock you're mud
Falling on your knees as if to pray
So silly wabbit said Elmer Fudd

Jump Jump Jump so what's the delay
Jump Jump Jump so the crowd can yell hooray
Jump Jump Jump

Smoke that cigarette one last time
And turn yourself to stone
See the sun trying to shine
Trying to change you from alone

Jump turn around go back don't do it
Jump don't want to go through with it

Play some more with the cigarettes
A blue clown from the circus
Finger painting with the ashes
Painting a picture of nervousness
Deciding you don't want to be a statistic
In the morning edition
Telling the crowd below to kiss off
Exhausted from emotion

Jump what's your delay jump hey come on Jump
Jump Jump Jump Jump we wanna see some action

Just Another Bar Band

(In which the artiste gets trounced for being cloudy)

(Artiste:) I want to write masterly
(Answer:) That's impossibility
(Artiste:) I want to write art—poetry
(Answer:) You know what that is?
That's crap, look, you need the hook
The hook

You can't write mysteriously
Words simple simplicity
Got to have that joyous glee
Got to be simple and that's that
Look you need the hook
The hook

Pollstar sez our market's growing
That means they ain't got zits showing
They're all under fourteen and not knowing
That our non-stop partying will
Stop too soon

(Stop and into a many hooked riff)

You can't write mysteriously
Words simple simplicity
Got to have that joyous glee
Got to be simple and that's that
Look you need the hook
The hook

Pollstar sez our market's growing
That means they ain't got zits showing
They're all under fourteen and not knowing
That our non-stop partying will
Stop too soon

(Artiste:) I can't seem to get it
The words are all but vapid
A heartless bent at winning
The hearts and minds of teens
With a sound that robs brain cells—like a crook
Look who needs that hook?
(Answer:) Look you need that hook—the hook.
Look

It's fun
It's frenetic
It's fu-fu-filling
It's fan freaking-tastic when it works

You can't write mysteriously
Words simple simplicity
Got to have joyous glee
Got to be simple and that's that
Look you need the hook
The hook

Just Need Love

(Lyrics by David L. Greenberg & Christiane D. Leach)

don't care how you treat me
my love love love will erase your hate
don't care your lies about me
my love love love will change your fate
eternal deep universal sweet
love love love

don't care how far you fall
my love love love will raise you up
don't care if you care at all
my love love love in a loving cup
whenever divine forever mine
love love love

don't care if you leave me
my love love love will fill in the wonder
don't care if you forget me
my love love love will find another
don't need you don't need me

(Break)

just need love as love can be the only thing that makes us bleed...
when it's gone

i don't care if you defeat me
my love love love back of my hand
i don't care if you mistreat me
my love love love will make a stand
incredible strong infernal wrong
love love love

don't care if it takes all night
my love love love will see me through
don't care got the rest of my life
my love love love regrets a few

love love love

don't care how you treat me
my love love love will erase your hate
don't care your lies about me
my love love love will change your fate
eternal deep universal sweet
love love love

(Break)

just need love as love can be the only thing that makes us bleed...
when it's gone

Christiane D., aka Chrissy D., aka Christiane Leach, who sings for IR as well as on her amazing album *Obliquity of the Ecliptic*, has been promising to collaborate on something. But like everyone else in the world who is underpaid and overworked, most likely she has been too busy to focus on much other than the stuff that pays the bills. When she dribbled some words into a Facebook post, I grabbed them and ran as fast as I could to a piece of blank paper to write us more of the same and then some more. This is it, a rough draft to be sure. Supposedly she WAS working on the music, or so she texted me. While she's not hammering out a tune for this, as again, it has been years since the last text about this lyrical, be sure to check out her album, or her tracks with our musical collective, IR::Indigenous Resistance.

Keeping Amused

Nothing is what it seems
Might be serious might be funny
You can never know what to think

You can play life in teams
With rules or razzle dazzle
Or just sit out with a drink

(Chorus:)
Grow on up keeping amused
You gotta laugh why?
Growing up is such a joke
Such a waste of time to cry

When things tumble apart
Glue dissolves love is lost
Solid ground begins to sink

Nothing is what it seems
Might be serious might be funny
You can never know what to think

(Chorus)

If everyone were less than smart
They'd laugh more think even less
Never even know when a joke stinks

Forget about follow the leader
See the door slamming shut
They'll tell you what to think

They'll sing your way to sleep

(Chorus)

The King Of Rock And Roll

Rambo's stone drunk, James Bond is dead
Even Bugs Bunny has lost his head
All the heroes fat and tan by the pool
Who can kick ass and still stay cool

The King Of Rock And Roll
sha-la-la-la-la-la (or shoobydoobyshoe)
The King Of Rock And Roll
be bop a lula
The King Of Rock And Roll
don't say maybe
The King Of Rock And Roll
say sayonara bay-uh-bee

We need the blinis, we need the beer
We need to fight off communist fear
Propaganda's pravda inside my head
Who can kick Kruschev outta his bed

The King Of Rock And Roll
sha-la-la-la-la-la (or shoobydoobyshoe)
The King Of Rock And Roll
be bop a lula
The King Of Rock And Roll
don't say maybe
The King Of Rock And Roll
say sayonara bay-uh-bee

Just a dial tone if you let freedom ring
Can't hang 'em high if you've got no string
We're all apes who've gone to hell
Who's gonna ring that Liberty Bell?

The King Of Rock And Roll
sha-la-la-la-la-la (or shoobydoobyshoe)
The King Of Rock And Roll
be bop a lula

The King Of Rock And Roll
don't say maybe
The King Of Rock And Roll
say sayonara bay-uh-bee

Another dotty ditty for the Red Elvises, this one taking on the role of body-double for the title track of the film Six String Samurai. They just lobbed in pre-recorded tracks from the Elvises back catalog for the film and never got around to creating a specific track to bang over the audience's heads at the start. And so, there was no lead-off track on the subsequent soundtrack album that we, Palm Pictures/Rykodisc, were releasing. The music was excellent, heaped with the Russky-Serf/Surf-Rock that was the Red Elvises stock in trade, but nothing to hang the film's apocalyptic kung-fu weirdness upon.

Wearing my product manager shoes and oversized (ill-fitting?) artistic hat, I knew a better way to market the flick post-release. Maybe help make it a cult film for the generations to come. The Elvises play a few hundred shows a year, every year before the flick's release and since, to the perfect potential audience: young samurai-anime-kung fu-loving, rocked and rolled, lust-filled lads. They would be essentially marketing the flick at all their shows if they sang my lyrics, hewing closer to the whacked-out plot of the film.

So I went ahead, again unsolicited, to write something. Again, never ever sung. Perhaps because Palm Pictures had the soundtrack album all sewn up and mint-ing a few thousand special edition singles to promote the film and the album, the Elvii must have tossed these words aside, as they've never appeared on any subsequent album. At least Tape Dave Music Co. has not collected any hun-dredths of a penny for this title. Yet. As the film has not even attained the lower rungs of cult status, singing my lyrics would have underscored yet another failed opportunity and exponentially nicer for me than it would have been for them.

The Last Time (Let's Pretend)

In the springtime
In the moontime
Falling all the way

Resolving madness
Opening happiness
Carrying your cross away

Away, away, away
Carrying your cross away

Does that cross weigh heavy
On your shoulder
Don't fall to being lazy
Try to get hold of
Falling all the way

Resolving madness
Opening happiness
Carrying your cross away

Away, away, away
Carrying your cross away

One crafted for Flying Island. Flying Island was the final incarnation of the jazz-rock band mentioned in the foreword. You did read that foreword, didn't you? Ray Smith, the lead guitarist at the time, wrote "Let's Pretend," a jamming instrumental piece with an Allman Brothers double-drummer kind-of chugging beat to it, which the one drummer, Bill Bacon, effortlessly achieved. After one of their practices, during my drive home through the backwoods of Stamford, the melody kept returning to me. Somewhere along the way, I had to find a place to pull over and stop to write this lyric, which, I thought, would fit the opening stanzas of Ray's tune. Did they ever sing it? If you have been paying attention and read the foreword as you should have, you would have answered an emphatic and resounding, "No!" Flying Island was an instrumental band with not one vocalist within 100 feet. A fact noted in the foreword that you should have read by now: a choice bit of knowledge that might have clued you, and most certainly me, in.

Lead Me On

Lead me lead me on
Take my hand
Lead me lead me on
Cannot see all is blurred
Lead me lead me on
Take my heart
Lead me lead me on
Put your best foot forward
Lead me on

Blues tie me down trip up my feet
As time marches on to a popular beat

Lessons of depressions blind my mind
Can't see how far I have fallen behind

Lead me lead me on
Take my hand
Lead me lead me on
Cannot see all is blurred
Lead me lead me on
Take my heart
Lead me lead me on
Put your best foot forward
Lead me on

(Bridge:)
Show me no more doubt
I need to have your love
Show me the way out
I want to hold your hand

Lead me lead me on
Take my hand
Lead me lead me on
Cannot see all is blurred
Lead me lead me on

Take my heart
Lead me lead me on
Put your best foot forward
Lead me on

No light at night is a heady dread
A simple hurdle simply stops me dead

Blues tie me down trip up my feet
As time marches on to a popular beat

Lead me lead me on
Take my hand
Lead me lead me on
Cannot see all is blurred
Lead me lead me on
Take my heart
Lead me lead me on
Put your best foot forward
Lead me on

Leaves Change

The leaves are falling onto the pavement
The smell of leaves burning
I'm not one to give into mistreatment
So to this town I'm not returning

The wind pushes me along down a path
Trees wave hello as I pass
Clouds glide overhead above the trees
Asking how long will I last

I'll last as long as you pass overhead
Long after you rain
It's sad but I'll be here after the trees
A parking lot terrain

I'll stumble along on new soles
Long after the rain
Feeling out new situations—finding the holes
Time will never tame

(Chorus:)
No—Time will never tame
Time will never change the madness
No you'll always have time to dream
Laugh at what tastes like happiness
(Repeat)

History isn't much of a reference
When history's changing
What was the tested past tense
Historians are rearranging

The future's not much to look at
With false prophets leaching
Their trusty Doomsday machine that
No one dares try stopping

The present is all I have to keep
But that isn't what it seems
What I need is someone to share my sleep
And learn about in my dreams

Birds hip hop and fly through trees
The smell of leaves burning
Sun filters through colored leaves
To my own life I'm returning

Stumbling along on new soles
Long after the pain
Feeling out new situations—finding the holes
Time will never tame

(Chorus:)
No—Time will never tame
Time will never change the madness
No you'll always have time to dream
Laugh at what tastes like happiness

(Repeat chorus + repeat chorus + repeat some more + then linger out
through the untamed madness of it all.)

Left Ear

Juniper surrounds his eyes
The blanket of night divulges his secrets
Telling her truths, amongst the lies
She loves his way with words she entreats it
Finally seeing eye to eye
Weaving tales beating rhythms heated
She sprinkles grass as he lies
As he story telling of past loves repeats it

Telling her night stories / Tells her night lies
Tells her night stories / Tells her white lies

As he lies / In the blanket of night

She listens to his provoking
As he prepares her along his course
Within feeling the heat of loving
A love smooth and easy a love unforced
Quiet laughter almost toying
Making a joke out of lover's remorse
She sprinkles grass while playing
With his shirt and pants and breath growing hoarse

Telling her night stories / Tells her night lies
Tells her night stories / Tells her white lies

As he lies / In the blanket of night

While writing, I understood this idea of a song was to be an acoustic folk thang, one the 1970s era King Crimson might have spun out; a bit fragile, a bit ragged, and then, at the chorus, all hell would break loose with Fripp electro chords flanging the song apart. Hal Freedman wrote it into a snappy salsa-inflected tune for his 1980s band, Frequency. It worked. So much for artistic intent. I learned to be open to anything after that one. Hal even had Blues Traveler John Popper, of all people, blow his harmonica, son, in the middle break of the very urban New Yorican salsa track. That worked as well. Though I doubt in any of his bands, Mr. Fripp would ever have incorporated that kind of harp.

Letter From China (Rock 2-4)

Pudgey sent me a letter from China
Sez now they're wearing black & white
Last week he scoured a market place
Found a house with a blinking red light

Find me an oriental woman
Find me an oriental woman
Find me an oriental woman
Find me one who can rock—2—4

Pudgey tried to eat a dinner with chopstix
Ended up with most on the floor
His hosts saw some egg on his face
He wiped it off and picked up a fork

Find me an oriental woman
Find me an oriental woman
Find me an oriental woman
Find me one who can rock—2—4

Went to the trial of the Gang of Four
Bunch a Chinese in a shouting match
Chinese just don't rock anymore
Their elevator music ain't worth a scratch

Find me an oriental woman
Find me an oriental woman
Find me an oriental woman
Find me one who can rock—2—4

Red brigades don't like this new disco
Want a little more cultural rev
But don't want a lottery to pick a wife
Want a rock—rock—rocking time in bed

Find me an oriental woman
Find me an oriental woman

Find me an oriental woman
Find me one who can rock—2—4

Pudgey sent me a letter from China
Postmarked at the bottom of the world
Sez he's buying up all the porcelain
But no luck finding a cracked China girl

Find me an oriental woman
Find me an oriental woman
Find me an oriental woman
Find me one who can rock—2—4

I nicked the line about the cracked China girl coming into my head from hearing
the Bowie song, probably listening to my Walkman on my long way home from
work at 53rd and Madison on down to the Village at West Tenth, clearing my
head for a night of creativity. From there, I let it bleed from my rock-addled
brain onto notebook paper. And how politically incorrect of me to use the term
"Oriental," Of course, you have to do all kinds of stupendously stupid stuff
like that in a big dumbass top ten wannabe rock song, Dontcha? Fuck yeah!
BTW, the Walkman reference dumps this lyric into the era of spandexed Arena
Rawkers, whose petrified remains one can usually excavate from the sediment of
the early 1980s. Or within the streams of Classic Rock Radio.

Live A Little

Put a little time away for yourself
Tuck hope in a well worn book
Writing in diaries is ever so tiring
Especially if that's all you do

Laundries and shopping days count
But they're not even yours
Fact you own a lot of nothing
Draining even what's left of life

Live a little
And you'll die a lot
Live a lot
And you'll think you won't die at all

Marry a man and marry his house
Love him at night sometimes work days
Defend your life with some soap operas
Get a sitter to play with baby

But who do you get to play with you
For you can't very well play with yourself
Get a pool boy get a gardener a cook
All the young dudes doing wonders for your health

Live a little
And you'll die a lot
Live a lot
And you'll think you won't die at all

Put a little time away for yourself
Memories if you choose to look
Old pictures, old letters, uninspiring
Reminders of what you didn't do

Wrestling demons go down for the count
But they're not even yours

Fact you own too much of nothing
Living even less of life

Live a little
And you'll die a lot
Live a lot
And you'll think you won't die at all

Live a lot
And you'll think you'll die laughing
If you ever can wrap your head around
Dying at all

Looking For Some

(Lyrics by David Greenberg & James Pakootas)

Looking for some action passion getting no traction
So you push harder
That's a non-starter
No matter how fast you run son there's no fun
Rushing the next corner
Crashing over and over

Looking for some is never done odds are against you

Looking for some action passion getting no traction
My wheels keep spinning as my chances keep passin'
So you push harder
That's a non-starter
No matter how fast you run son there's no fun
Rushing the next corner
Each line you cross is only the next border.

They say God can move mountains, I can't even lift a Boulder.
Crashing over and over, standing shoulder to shoulder
The only ones who fail forward get ahead when it's all over
So go and tell whoever that sent you
Looking for some is never done odds are against you
But if you keep going you'll do more
than you were ever even meant to

Fail forward don't live in your head
Look for some sensibility
Some reason and rhyme
Depression may fill you with dread
Look for some sense of wonder
Some time to feeling just fine

Love Is A Many Splintered Thing

love is a many splintered thing
a sliver for you
a sliver for me
a sliver in your eye
when you try to leave
love, oh yes love,
love is a many splintered thing

love is a many splintered thing
you say you hate me
you say alot of things
you can't leave until you
gimme back the diamond ring
love, oh yes love
love is a many splintered thing

love is a many splintered thing
there's nothing left
except hate in your heart
will this really end when
death do us part
love, oh yes love
love is a many splintered thing

love is a many splintered thing
you've ruined my life
you've fucked my head
even so, bay-uh-be
can you please (pause) come back to bed
you've ruined my live
you've fucked my head
do it again bayuhbe
yes, do it again bayuhbe
love is a many splintered thing

don't it hurt?

Love Love Love

(Lyrics by David Greenberg & Christiane D. Leach)

don't care how you treat me
my love love love will erase your hate
don't care your lies about me
my love love love will change your fate
eternal deep universal sweet
love
love
love
don't care how far you fall
my love love love will raise you up
don't care if you care at all
my love love love in a loving cup
whenever divine forever mine
love
love
love
don't care if you leave me
my love love love will fill in the wonder
don't care if you forget me
my love love love will find another
don't need you don't need me

[break] just need love as love can be the only thing that makes us
bleed...
when it's gone

i don't care if you defeat me
my love love love back of my hand
i don't care if you mistreat me
my love love love will make a stand
incredible strong infernal wrong
love
love
love
don't care if it takes all night
my love love love will see me through

don't care got the rest of my life
my love love love regrets a few
love
love
love
don't care how you treat me
my love love love will erase your hate
don't care your lies about me
my love love love will change your fate
eternal deep universal sweet
love
love
love

[break] just need love as love can be the only thing that makes us
bleed...
when it's gone

Low Rent Rhumba (The)

Come on up to my room
Come on up to my room
Come on up to my room (Let me show you around)
Come on up to my room (Let me show you around)
Come on up to my room (Let me show you around)
Theres' a lamp there's the teevee
There's a stove and the hi-fidelity

Come on up to my room
You won't find anything new
Anything brand-spanking white
It's my philosophy of living
And because the money's tight
That's the low-rent rhumba

Let me show you around
I've friends living in white (rooms)
Metal chairs that are all alike
Cuisinarts that won't start
Rooms so clean you don't dare fart
(or: Rooms so clean you'll become art)
That's not living—thats hi-tech

Who needs hi-tech huh?
Who needs hi-tech huh?
Who needs hi-tech huh?
When you've got low rent low low rent

Let me show you around
When you dance to hi-tech
Your avant garde goes all awreck
Be a machine from head to toe
And dance hypnotically slow
That's not living—it's a pain in the neck

Who needs hi-tech huh?
Who needs hi-tech huh?

Who needs hi-tech huh?
When you've got low rent—low low rent

Come on up to my room
Come on up to my room
Come on up to my room (Let me show you around)
Come on up to my room (Let me show you around)
Come on up to my room (Let me show you around)

There's a chair theres a divan
There's a brunette theres a blond
There they go again on my teevee
And how sweet is low rent in hi-fidelity

Low low rent in hi-fidelity

(Bridge:)
In hi-tech kitchenettes
They never find the girls go wet
Or sing like some Modettes
In this years cut of shirts
They never find the love that hurts
Finding a life of crepes suzettes
Metal and white bedroom sets

Turnstile Frigidare romances
An afternoon of slow dances
A twilight of trim choices
Hey all the low rent girls and boys sez
Come on up to my room

Come on up to my room
Come on up to my room
Come on up to my room (Let me show you around)
Come on up to my room (Let me show you around)
Come on up to my room (Let me show you around)
Theres' a lamp there's the teevee
There's a stove and the hi-fidelity

LNFS Superdupermarket Remix

*(Preliminary lyric for remix of IR/Asian Dub Foundation track for IR26.
Lyrics by David Greenberg & Christiane D. Leach)*

always fear you make it clear a living nightmare
wish to erase bitterest taste this is nowhere
find our true face find our true place our somewhere

this land is not for sale
put us in jail
you will fail
full sail
airports shopping malls superdupermarkets
powerlines it's about time you find out mine is mine
stealing is a god-damn gawdawful crime
this land is our land this land is our land
this land is not yours to own
e-t phone home
you're the alien here
we're gonna be your fear
fear us dust to dust as
though you must
you must fail
you will fail
hear our tale
this land our land is not for sale

always fear you make it clear dreams frightmares
wish to erase bitterest taste getting somewhere
find our true face this is our true place this this this
land is not for sale

Original tracks: "This Land Is Not For Sale" is on Asian Dub Foundation's
A History Of Now & the "Fatta Atenco Emergency Instrumental Remix" on
IR::Indigenous Resistance's *IR25 Dubversive*.

Miami Heat

(Chorus:)
Gotta hideaway gotta hideaway gotta hideaway
Turn your head away
I'll try to get away get a way outta here
I feel old too old to be again on the run
I feel old too old to be under the aim of a gun

I can't find any shadows to stand in / In this Miami heat
On my tail hired Cubans / Turning up Miami's heat
I owed a lot of money I found out / Dickweed loan sharker
My lover stole everything I had / Might be finer with a minor in
Either one of those Caroliners

(Chorus)

Used to have a bitching Camaro / But I had to pawn it
Bitch stole all my dineros / I got burned dammit
My lover really done me good / Just loved the money more
Now there's hired guns in the hood / I know what's in store

(Chorus)

Not even thirty and I'm feeling old
My life's like a cheap detective novel
If you're not a corpse you're in deep shit trouble

(Chorus)

I can't find any shadows to stand in
In this Miami heat
I can't find anywhere to lay low in
In this Miami heat

Miracle Mile

Jogging down the miracle mile
One step two step on my tippy toes
Skip along at triple speed always wave hello

Jogging down the miracle mile
Used to get depressed way too often
My hardened heart...uh...softened

Jogging down the miracle mile
Walking on water water into wine
Ordinary miracles not miracles of mine

Jogging down the miracle mile
Love was my enemy love was my hate
Love is now my very important date

Jogging down the miracle mile
Fail at first give it one more try
Every step I take I'm glad to be alive

Jogging down the miracle mile
Passing my streets passing by petty talk
Passing by cross moods filling up cross walks

Jogging down the miracle mile
Don't use the well worn path the beaten track
Running forward don't be afraid to run back

Jogging down the miracle mile
When things went wrong found a need to fight
Made up my mind don't you know I'm right

Jogging down the miracle mile
There's a new miracle every other step
My pockets full with all I can get

Jogging down the miracle mile

Nothing can get close to test my limit
Gonna rack up more miracles per minute

(The suntanned-boys chorus takes over we slow fade out:)
Jogging down the miracle mile
Jogging down the miracle mile
Jogging down the miracle mile
Jogging down the miracle mile
Jogging down the miracle mile
Jogging down the miracle mile
Jogging down the miracle mile
Jogging down the miracle mile

Morning Before Sunrise

The fog lays close to the ground
The trees stand silent—guards of the night
Muffled whispered sound
Echos from over the pavement—twin headlights

I'm tired I've been driving all night and I'll be driving after the sunrise
The girl who hates her name and I are breaking all ties
We were just clouds blown by the wind now we don't surmise
That our plans can't change we can always rewrite them

I glance at her laying close to me
She is dreaming—a time till waking
I can think of nothing but she
She is sleeping—so distracting

We're living in the morning before sunrise
Where the darkness hides no lies
We're living in the morning before sunrise
Day undressing the night

I'm tired I've been driving all night and I'll be driving after the sunrise
The girl who hates her name and I are breaking all ties
We were just clouds blown by the wind now we don't surmise
That our plans are in stone we can always rewrite them

Being in love is no surprise
The night seems to be—slowly ending
The morning before the sunrise
Awakes the birds—who start singing

We're living in the morning before the sunrise

Mousie

Mechanically waiting looking for some shoes
Scuffling footsteps to rest against the blues
Keep them moving as not to get bored
What's the matter why is she getting sore

Is it that you're an hour late
Or is it the pettiness that she hates
Or the contagious blues getting her bored
She yells "Goodbye" and slams the door

You're a letterman a football hero an old cliché
While you ponder watching a rerun of Anita O'Day
Expecting a miracle of instant respect or so you pray
You have to give in to be forgiven just don't say

That it's her fault you're an hour late
Scuffing the Persian rug
Keep your eyes bouncing from the hate
And kiss it off with a shrug

Blissfully repeating of your witty charm
While helping out doing nothing but harm
Keep on your toes you're a good target
Throwing verbal darts she won't let you forget

That you're ancient in every single way
A mouse never once been a prey
She's a cat not letting you get away

She bites deeply into your arm-chair quarterback
Never once giving you a chance to fight back
Like a fly gently alighting on cooked meat
She touches on the subject of your being a cheat

You're a letterman a football hero an old cliche
While you ponder the final defeat and what to say
Expecting a miracle of instant respect or so you pray
You have to give in to be forgiven you don't want to stay

MRI

They find nothing in my gut
I'm drawn and quartered
Spent and saddened
Disease and sickness let's slam this sad book shut

Even my dreams drain me
I'm running to the abyss
Worried something they missed
Is what's rearranging and changing what was me [the real me]

Oncology oncology you've gotten the better of me
The light in my step
The wit in my charm
I used to be funny now I'm just alarmed

I used to wonder why they called them boobs
In junior high they laughed at tits
MBAs can't seem to find my eyes
Up here buddy read my lips
Never in my wildest dreams could I guess
How they make me feel like shit

They find nothing in my gut
I'm drawn and quartered
Spent and saddened
Disease and sickness let's slam this sad book shut

Even my dreams drain me
I'm running to the abyss
Worried something they missed
Is what's rearranging and changing what was me [the real me]

Oncology oncology you've gotten the better of me
The light in my step
The wit in my charm
I used to be funny now I'm just alarmed

Mud

i sit watching disco queens go by
they come like bad dreams of last night
they say: each only a grain of sand in a puddle of mud
they say: each only living in cubicles workers in the hive

they're so smart

i think of moondog today
listening to what mr krishna has to say
they say: each only a grain of sand in a puddle of mud
they say: each only living in cubicles workers in the hive

they're so smart

overhearing bishops kneel to pray
and flushing meadow pilgrims hailing cabs to shea
they say: each only a grain of sand in a puddle of mud
they say: each only living in cubicles workers in the hive

they're so smart

the rainbow palette of clothes sparkle
the expense of welfarees is remarkable
they say: each only a grain of sand in a puddle of mud
they say: each only living in cubicles workers in the hive

they're so smart

the flamenco kings with their castanets and cockroached kitchenettes
the police procrastinate and are taken aback at the surprising lack
of fatalities or so they say

they say: each only a grain of sand in a puddle of mud
they say: each only living in cubicles workers in the hive

they're so smart

the cloth priests rise religiously
and soon-to-be-wedded June brides matrimoniously
marry the street in haste as if to flee
the daguerreotyped lives of their mother-in-laws to be

they say: each only a grain of sand in a puddle of mud
they say: each only living in cubicles workers in the hive
they're so smart
i wish I were that smart
i wish I were that smart
i wish I were that smart
but I'm not that depressed

Mumm's The Word

Thirsty for a little action / Hungry for some illegal thrill
Want a place where you can speak easy / With plenty of time to kill

Drink away the depression / Dance a nickel dance or two
You can flirt with all the big boys / Take one home when you're through

(Girl chorus:)
There's no front way come in the back way
The up and up is on the sly
Be discrete when on the street
Passing coppers and the F.B.I.
Shhhhhhh—Mumm's the word

Only smile at the showgirls / Don't let 'em kiss and tell
They all have jealous boyfriends / The kind that shoot to kill

(Girl chorus:) I'm free and I'm easy
(Boy chorus:) She has expensive tastes
(Girl chorus:) None of my men are single
(Boy chorus:) None of her diamond's paste

(Boy chorus:)
There's no front way come in the back way
The up and up is on the sly
Be discrete when on the street
Passing coppers and the F.B.I.
Shhhhhhh—Mumm's the word

Written for an Off-Off-Broadway musical a friend was scripting and produc-
ing, although the composer he finally hired for the musical wanted HER lyrics
and HER music to be "The Show," and this one was left forgotten. In the gutter.
Funny, the composer's lyric for her "Mumm's The Word" theme lifted more than
a scad of visuals straight from this lyric with not a whit of attribution by all those
involved. Not that I didn't cop more than a few ideas from too many afternoon
matinees of Film Noir flicks on our B&W Motorola back in our TV room on
Parade Hill Road in the '60s. Still, dang it, I would have loved to see my name in
Playbill. Since the musical never found any backers, no one else did either.

New Day Drowning

looking for a new day
anybody have one in their back pocket?
this one's dragging me down
so useless I just wanna hock it

looking for a new day
one bright and shiny and halfway to hope
even settle for a dull one
a little bit tarnished a slippery slope

been in this hole so long the river's flowing over my head
one two three i'm drowning
been under water so long my life's dissolving its thread
one two three i'm drowning

looking for bright clouds
at least the storm'll be a dying dervish
cut off it's tap tap tap shoes
laugh in his face he's so girlish

looking for bright clouds
cause that'll mean the haze'll lift me
don't mind being in a fog
set me adrift in a calming sea

one two three
one two one
one two three
one two two
one

looking for a new day
got one I could beg borrow or steal
you'll get it back just
will be a little used a little less real

looking for a new day

anybody have one in their back pocket?
this one's dragging me down
so so useless I just wanna stop it
been in this hole so long the river's flowing over my head
one two three i'm drowning
just want to shut my eyes go back to my warm bed
one two three i'm drowning

Night Club

The saxophone wails
Crying for recognition wailing for love
Love to get a table
Living in depression the people shove

Smoke curls up
And you waft a circle around
Trying to push
Away interested fools closing down

Smoke curls up
When you finally turn around
The saxophone unfurls
Delivering a most bitter put-down

My hope falters
Waiting for recognition waiting for love
The saxophone wails
Crying for recognition crying for you

Your eyes wander
Never staying in one place
Your hopes are high
That this night won't be erased

Your eyes wander
A flutter with wonder and distaste
From way up high
How can love ever reach that place

My eyes fear
That you, can't you see any one in love

No Bikini Atoll

Ooooooo oooogling / I'm a oogling the girl
Ooooooo oooogling / I'm a oogling the girl
Who's not wearing as much as one stitch of cloth
Ooooooo crazy

(Chorus:)
She was the only girl with no bikini at all
She was the only girl with no bikini at all
All the other girls would promise and leave you waiting
(break)
She was the only girl with no bikini at all
No bikini no bikini no bikini at all

Ooooooo honey / Why don'tcha be my gal
Ooooooo honey / Why don'tcha be my gal
I've always had a spot for girls with skin so soft
Ooooooooo crazy

(Chorus)

Ooooooo surfs up / Let's go ballistic bayuhbe
Ooooooo surfs up / Let's go ballistic bayuhbe
And stay up late trying to detonate

Woobopaloobop / Whambamthankyoumaam
Ooooooo nuclear

(Chorus)

Those were the days! A great and wondrous time when America's brainpower
and superior technology were aimed at rendering the world a peaceful place
whelmed in the logic of mutually assured obliteration and ultimate disintegration
of life as we know it. Ever wonder what a Cold War-era novelty tune would sound
like released on the heels of those A-bomb tests in the South Pacific? That is,
if anyone back then had the temerity (or a supreme lack of propriety) to write a
dopey pop lyric with such a sobering subtext? Who could write such a dumb,
callous, insensitive thing? Well, wonder no more.

Nothing Left

So tell me what to do
What's that you say?
Can't find what's true
I'm so tired, I'm a fucking cliché

There's nothing left
There's nothing left
There's nothing left
Where's the little old me?

Chipped at my soul
Nothing's full
Nothing's whole
I'm so spent, so throw me away

There's nothing left
There's nothing left
There's nothing left
Where's what was left of me?

Had miracles by the pocketful
Had life by the balls
Whirled my dervish I had it all
It's not half empty not even half full
Spent
Kicked down
Dragged along
Empty as that bitter cold morning
Empty as the signs I had never seen
Empty as the unheard warning
Empty and blind and deaf and mean
There's nothing left
There's nothing left
There's nothing left
Where's the belief?
Where's the relief?
Can't find what I thought was underneath

Not Moving

Not moving not moving at all
If I don't move I'll never fall
No life no life on the line
Then I don't lose I'll always find
High wire high wire balancing
Can't live by death defying
Not moving not moving at all
If I don't move I'll never fall

No Way Nothing

The coffee reservoir is low
Train of thought is moving slow
Got that sour feeling in tow
No chance of being in the know
No chance of nothing
And nothing comes from nothing
Don't you know

And nothing comes from nothing
Don't you know

Now/Then

there was a time maybe last week maybe yesterday
you said something that i forgot but you said that was okay
there was a time maybe the day after the other day
when you gave me the glance that said no fucking way

let's get back to where we were
let's get back to understanding
let's get back to being so damn sure

to dream the dream and tame the nightmares
to slip between the now and the anywheres
to fall for each other and try to not defend
all the rootless rumors we hang on and befriend

let's get back to where we were
let's get back to understanding
let's get back to being so damn sure

to dream the dream and tame the nightmares
to slip between the now and the anywheres
to fall for each other and try to not defend
all the rootless rumors we hang on and befriend

there was a time maybe last week maybe yesterday
you said something that i forgot but you said that was okay
there was a time maybe the day after the other day
when you gave me the glance that said no fucking way

On Catsteps

You look tired and ready to sleep
But also very upset and trying to keep
Your problems tucked far away
Lighting a fire under them
Hoping they fly away

No matter how you try to see
What was a past love is still a memory
Tugging at strands of your brain
Weaving a jumble of macramé
Nothing will ever be the same

I'm holding back from starting
Anything you're not sure of beginning
I'm restraining not trying to rush
Not trying to overload your mind
Weeping sleeping screaming—hush

You feel guilty for keeping me waiting
While you sort things out—don't worry I'll still be here
I know how hard it is for you
I've felt that pain—all that you're pressed to bear

I'm not as good a poet
As I wish I were and know it
I can't read people's feelings—Try to write but not read
As well as I wish I could
So I won't know when your heart's healing

So on carefully controlled catsteps
Our relationship walks—I'm standing on caution
I'm asking you when I can
Be very loose and easy—when can I stroll in

On Parade

Into the car got my stuff
Into the car
now fellas don't get rough

I know I'm on my way
My Daddy says I can't stay
He says that my eyes are in the stars
I know that he means I'll go far

Now fellas my bags are packed I'm ready to go
But really guys I washed my face my skins all aglow

We have our press passes
And goodies from Mom
We have our Neon sunglassses
Like Elton John

Like wow

Into the car got my stuff
Into the car
now fellas don't get rough

That must be my neon I lost mine on Sunset and Vine
It must be my neon it just has to be mine

Now fellas like wow

Now now fellas
Like Elton John oh wow
We're on parade
Just marching on by
Zippered up ready to fight
C'mon join us guys

The blade suited misers blazing into technocrat glory
While little Billy repeats his story for the second time

The freon's running out of my dribbling mouth
I remember losing it with the neon on Sunset and Vine

We're on parade
NBC's here to record the story
We're on parade
We're National Stars just not as gory
We're on parade
Hey Mom hello can you see me

Now fellas
Now now fellas oh wow

On The Road

The sun flickers and dies like a prayer candle drowning
In it's own pool of wax
Clouds whisper and change to colors and disappear
Fade to tonal ranges of black

People sit in their loneliness cafés and drown themselves
With what seems coffee
Waiting and staring and not really caring
Where they seem to find their money

Dragging driftless
Thinking of past loves
Broken hearts
Laughing that
It didn't hurt them
Laughing

People sit in their loneliness cafés and drown themselves
With what seems coffee
Waiting and staring and not really caring
Where they seem to lose their money

On Top

(On top) Want to yell out loud
(On top) 'Cause I feel so proud
(On top) My outlook's sunny
(On top) I'm like everybody

Hey Ma I'm sitting on top of the world
(Everybody's up here with me)
Hey Ma I'm sitting on top of the world
(Getting down's gonna be tricky)

Hey Ma I'm sitting on top of the world

(On top) It's a brand new day
(On top) No more yesterdays
(On top) Gonna walk on air
(On top) Dancing everywhere

Hey Ma I'm sitting on top of the world
(Everybody's up here with me)
Hey Ma I'm sitting on top of the world
(Getting down's gonna be tricky)

Hey Ma I'm sitting on top of the world

(On top) Want to yell out loud
(On top) 'Cause I feel so proud
(On top) My outlook's sunny
(On top) I'm like everybody

Hey Ma I'm sitting on top of the world
(Everybody's up here with me)
Hey Ma I'm sitting on top of the world
(Getting down's gonna be tricky)
Hey Ma I'm sitting on top of the world
(It makes me feel so good)
Hey Ma I'm sitting on top of the world
(Just like I know I should)

Hey Ma I'm sitting on top of the world
(Ready to lend a helping hand)
Hey Ma I'm sitting on top of the world
(Strike up the marching band)

(Again, background choruses here of "on top," but this time it should be a lot of cute and excitable female singers, more than enough to take the song over the, yup, over the top.)

One More Rung

Am I just one more rung on your ladder
Am I just one more rung to take you higher
Am I just your marionette you pulled the strings
Am I just your marionette to get you things

You needed me as your ladder
So you stood on my back
You needed to lift yourself higher
I had to stop I can't take the weight

You needed to use me so that's what you did
Use me then throw me away I no longer fit

Don't ask your friends to do something that will profit you

(Repeat from the top)

Now I feel like a clown with a smile painted with a smile with a with a
With a smile painted over a frown

One Way (In The Tunnel)

There's only one way
One way in the tunnel
It's to Love
Love and serve the people
There's only one way
One way in the tunnel
It's to serve
Serve and live the person

His images abound and the multitude of sounds
It's as if you never left and never even came

There's only one way
One way in the tunnel
And that's to Love
Serve and Live your person
For the overflow
It is starting to rain
You're the only person
The only one who felt only pain

There's no pressure at all eat anything you want
Everything just multiplies nothing ever dies

Bisecting the tunnel is a double line
Never ever cross it if you really want to save your mind

There's only one way
One way in the tunnel
Once you get beneath
All the shredded tinsel
There's only one way
One Way in the tunnel
And that's to remember where you are

One way one way
One way one way

There's one light but that's only at the end
There's only the one white light at the end

Remember it's a tunnel
And not a cave
It's more like a funnel
Just remember to behave
His images abound
And the multitude of sounds
It's as if you never left
And never even came

The Peon Dance

You need to keep your world straight and simple
I need to write your stupid script
Should I have been cute shown my dimples
Smiling like some toothsome drip

I can you know
I need the chance
I can dance the Peon Dance

Trains run on time letters get mailed
We're the ones who leave the paper trail
We bake the dough we get out on bail
Both sides of the bars we run the jail

We can you know
We wear the pants
When we dance the Peon Dance

Order us to get what you want
Savor your life as a dilettante
You just might end your days
Washing dishes in a restaurant.

This plea may mean nothing to you
But it means all the world to me

Step on us as you get bolder
Stamp out our fire to make us colder
Lean on us as you get older
Weight of the world is on our shoulder

I can you know
I need the chance
I can dance the Peon Dance
I have to know
Do I have the chance
Have to dance the Peon Dance

The People-People

Night toppled steeplechase / Seems to come around
And the debased debonaires / After work step down

Trolley Car riding down your tracks
And then riding up your back
Trolley Car he's five minutes late
And the trainman's dressed as an ape
Oh Trolley Car

He rides down the middle of the city
Seeing the sights from a window that's dirty
The train makes all the lights turn red
And now from the inside of his head

Night toppled steeplechase / Seems to come around
And the suitcased millionares / Watch their step down

And the Cape it broke off
Provincetown I think it still exists
It was slowly eaten away
The Dunes weren't big enough to resist

At the Marconi Station
He couldn't wire any explanation
Besides he was in its way

And now the noonday sun
Instead of land shimmers on the waters

It wasn't that easy
It wasn't that hard
Alright where's the fire
Let's see your I.D. Card
The dude in the white top hat
Has his finger aimed at your back
What he says has gotta go
And when you do it do it slow

And the People-People people yea / Watch the day as it trolleys by
The People-People people oh yea / Always waiting for some sky

In their grey studded overalls / They have to turn people down
But really most of all / They're not allowed to frown

Getting loose to do some preaching
With their chants and supposed teachings

And the Guru
Can lead the life he must lead
For all of us
Pay top price for orchestra seats
Oh the Guru

Guru in his Fujicolor® overalls
Beckoning us near
When everyone is close enough
Fills his eyes with induced fear
Oh the Guru

He drops down to the fountain
And hits his head against the steel
When the water finally comes out
Nothing left for him to feel
Oh the Guru

And the People-People people yea / In their suits of grey
The People-People people oh yea / Are very strict in what they say

Night toppled steeplechase / Seems to come around
And the greysuited millionares / Watch their step down

People Person

(Chorus:)
I'm a people person give me that human touch
I'm a people person in the zone don't need that much
I'm a people person always ready to begin
I love to love a person don't need no mannequin

Don't do it on the phone no-no don't do it alone
That thing called sexting? Throw that dog a bone

(Chorus)

Magazines you don't need staples'll make you bleed
I'll show you some poses you'll never ever believe

(Chorus)

Face to face and toe to toe a glory to behold
Gonna be a bumpy ride you better grab ahold

(Chorus)

Don't think of it as lust love me as you must
But if you love another woman I'll grind you into dust

(Chorus)

So I'm dressed to kill and so emotional
If you can get passed all that I'm so electrical

(Chorus)

Pillow talk is fine on your pillow or on mine
Heavenly poems of love will always blow my mind

(Chorus)

Show n' tell n' kiss n' rave

Tell me what you really crave
But don't ever tell me
Never ever tell me
Never ever ever ever

Tell me

How to

Behave

(Chorus)

I'm a people person, people do right by me
People better do right — by me

Driving home and listening to the China Moses' Dinah Washington-inspired al-
bum, *This One's For Dinah*, I was transported into a nightclubbing mood with the
bopping blues beat and retro sassy-ness of it all. Then, I conjured up a bigger-
than-life singer treating some unsuspecting businessman in the front row of that
same nightclub as if he was her toy, sexing him up with innuendos, then having
him melt into his seat humiliated at ever thinking he could have his way with her.
Yeah, a tad retro, but I was born in the Fifties and daydreamed of being 007 and
hanging with Dino and Frank, even while a fanboy to FZ and Motown.

I "heard" some of the lyrics to this on my way home from work and had to park
on the side of the road, yet again, to pull out a pen from somewhere under my
seat and, then, my notebook somewhere else in the car. Imagine that nightclub
with China singing this one, or her mom, Dee Dee Bridgewater, or just about any
of those few bigger-than-life singers: the very few who possess that full-bore
confidence, that natural, honest sexiness and who could put just about any pig of
a man in their rightful place with just one smoldering look.

Philo-Sophie

I've got to make my song heavy
So people will listen to me
I've got to make my song heavy
I can't use no philosophy

I've got make my song heavy
So I can be rich with money
I want my song so heavy
So all my rhymes rhyme with "E"

Oh my heavy song
Heavy Heavy song

Can you feel my guitar bass 'n' drums
It's getting heavier man here it comes

I will be myself in my heavy song
Wherever I go it's myself that sings
I'll write 'bout Doctors and Broadway Dreams

If I want to recognized
Make me a shitload of money
Heavy heavy gotta be heavy
It's a mother that necessity

I won't be myself in my heavy song
Wherever I go I'll ripoff things
I'll write 'bout drugs and Mississippi Queens

I've got to make my song heavy
So people will listen to me
So people will understand me
So people will give money to me
Can't wait for all the money
I'll be so very rich you see
So I've got to be so heavy
So I can't use philosophy

Pimms!

You need a force of nature
To bat back all the haters
Especially when you're feeling sunk
Or flat on your ass wasted drunk

Or you need another drink
To clear your head to think
Especially when you're in that funk
& pissants are once again spouting junk

Leave me alone leave me alone
Don't need much
Give me my Pimms oh my pimms
And a crutch

The taste of it is heaven
The taste of it is heaven
Oh heaven I tell ya, though it's hell to pay
When it goes away
Oh! kay....

You need a force of nature
If not now then later
Especially when seeing in twos
Or you've once again made the nightly news

Leave me alone leave me alone
Don't need much
Give me my Pimms or a whisky
That would be clutch

You need a force of nature
To batt back all the haters
Especially when you're feeling sunk
Or flat on your ass wasted drunk

When you need another drink

To help you when you think
Especially when you're in that funk
& pissants are once again spouting junk

(The Adele-like break:)
About you
About you
About you
& pissants are running amuck
About you

What the fuck

Pick Up Stix

Cold beat is rhythm of my life/A frozen pie slice of life

Android made my breakfast
Made my bed
Wrote the paper
Keeps me fed
Android plays my drums
Sings my songs
Makes me feel
Like I belong
Something's left out something's wrong

Throw away the microchips and pick up sticks (x2)
Play the drums for a burning beat

Android washes the dishes
Cleans the sink
Reads my books
Helps me think
Android pays the bills
Embezzles the funds
Plans my parties
Plans my fun
Something's left out something's wrong

Throw away the microchips and pick up sticks (x2)
Play the drums for a burning beat

Android packed his bag
Said goodbye
Bought for him
His ticket to ride

Throw away the microchips and pick up sticks (x? through fade out)

––––––––––

In the 1980s, before my videos for Rubber Rodeo hit MTV and way before those
same videos were Grammy-nominated, our company, Second Story Televi-

sion, was clamoring for more work in the biz. SST partner and producer David Brownstein connected with Danny Gottlieb (drummer in the Pat Metheny Group at the time) and Joy Askew (singer/keyboardist soon to be with Laurie Anderson) to create a spec video script for a drum manufacturer. The video would then become a soft marketing piece. It was that kind of under-the-radar spec we even had to come up with and record the "hit" song before the suits would consider funding the production. While everyone was pondering where and how to begin, I had the idea of this human drummer stuck in an Iron Man-like android suit and then—throwing away the microchips—ripping the suit off to finally play the drums in "honest" analog. I wrote these lyrics.

The budget for this high-concept idea could never lead to a cheap production, even with someone else's money. So that Iron-Man thing was never scripted. I left SST sometime soon after the song was recorded by Danny Caccavo with Gottlieb and Askew's music and performances. It's on a cassette somewhere in my basement. The drum manufacturer lost interest, but SST did produce a video of the song later on, which Brownstein directed. I think that's in my basement as well. Brownstein somehow found a copy. They don't have basements out there in Los Angeles, so there was probably less history for him to root through. It now resides on YouTube under David's moniker, DJ Trotsky. If you google "Pick Up Sticks ft. Danny Gottlieb," you can see Danny and everyone else in full '80s hair and colorific neon fashion. It's a definite trip.

By the way, in case you were wondering, the Rubber Rodeo short-form video of *Scenic Views* lost to David Bowie's video release, *David Bowie*, at the 27th Grammy Awards in 1984. When the band and I walked in for the pre-show awards ceremony, which took to the stage hours before the telecast Grammy Awards, we passed by the public already waiting in the stands. This was the time slot when they awarded those not-ready-for-prime-time categories, of which we were one. The early risers were waiting to view and yell at the Rock Royalty and not some New Wave Cowboy Band whose songs, by that time in the release cycle, had already fallen off both the radio and MTV playlists or probably slotted into the late evening slots of College FM radio, if played at all.

Someone in the crowd yelled at us, thinking we might be famous: Who are you? I remember responding with a hearty yell of: Nobody. Or maybe I want to remember that I had something to say. Though these many years later, I have a hazy review of the scene. Perhaps it wasn't me with that quip. I can also see Gary Leib, Rubber Rodeo's keyboard player, yelling that NOBODY! back to them as a joke, we all headed away and into the Dorothy Chandler Pavillion, high with the hope of those great possibilities we imagined for our futures.

And R.I.P. Gary, most assuredly making Heaven a joyful and sillier locale.

The Policeman's Polka

You play numbers you roll dice
You haven't been very nice
We call this the Policeman's Polka

You polka him he polka you
We polka you down to Police HQ
We call this the Policeman's Polka

You polka him you polka us
We throw you in the big black bus
We call this the Policeman's Polka

We make you talk we make you plea
We lock you up and hide the key
We call this the Policeman's Polka

(Chorus:)
We make you dance we make you sing
We make you sing we make you dance
We make you sing until you dance
With us you don't stand the chance
We call this the Policeman's Polka

We drag you down to City Hall
Don't forget your one free call
We call this the Policeman's Polka

You complain your face is marred
Hey this ain't the Scotland Yard
We call this the Policeman's Polka

Go to court it's plain to see
The judge'll give you leniency
We call this the Policeman's Polka

(Insert chorus here and repeat until all the polka is gone from your blood
or the blood from your brain or the vodka has all but been drained from
the bottles that were in your freezer.)

Political Song nr. 24

Hey did you fill your quota today
Take down the names of the people who voted "yea"
Are you what you are or a product of what they say
After it's over and they've lost are you going to stay

Did you protest for the Indigenous
Pass leaflets out for the poor
If you decide to run for President
Knock on your own door

You in your blue jean uniform
Attacking the middle class norm
Yourself conforming to the regiment
Longhair in Levis® overalls

Straighten out your own ideas
Make sure their your own and no one elses
Instead of singing start writing
About the assholes who blow up houses

Hey did you fill your quota today
Take down the names of the people who voted "yea"
Are you what you are or a product of what they say
After it's over and they've lost are you going to stay

Did you protest for the Indigenous
Pass leaflets out for the poor
If you decide to run for President
Knock on your own door

The Pressure Scheme

When I say there is too much pressure
You have to say there is too much pressure
When I say that it's too hot
If we say it loud enough
If we say it fast enough
It won't do a goddamn thing

Pressure pressure pressure / Much too much pressure

If you want to follow me round
If I want to follow you round
If you want to wear my shirts
If I want to wear your dirt
If we do it fast enough
If we do it meaningful
It won't mean a goddamn thing

Pressure pressure pressure / Much too much pressure

We can do a lot of chitter chatter
We can teach the kiddies better
We can break down doors
We can fight to end all wars
We can do this we can do that
We can nick-knack paddywack
It won't do a goddamn thing

Pressure pressure pressure / Much too much pressure

When I say there's too much pressure (sit beside me)
When I say there's too much pressure (lay atop me)
When I say that it's too hot (move a little)
When I say that it's too hot (move a lot)
If we do it fast enough
If we do it loud enough
That's the pressure scheme

Pressure pressure pressure / Oooo the pressure

Questions I Forgot (To Ask)

My mind's a blank
Totally clean slate
Sinking? I've sank
Feeling like a fake

Getting nowhere
Traffic jams find me
Bitter? Don't care
Shoot me in my sleep

Sadness taught my spoons to bend
Hate to see the end of the day
Nights've got my wounds to mend
Speechless when I intend to say
I need to learn to love again
I need to learn to love again
I need to learn to find the end
And begin again

Too close I swear
To settle for less
Emotions? Laid bare
Destroyed none-the-less

Get over this
Don't know how I can
Careless? A mess
Drowning in quicksand

Sadness taught my spoons to bend
Hate to see the end of the day
Nights've got my wounds to mend
Speechless when I intend to say
I need to learn to love again
I need to learn to love again
I need to learn to find the end
And begin again

(Bridge:)
Can't give myself one damn ounce of mercy
One sweet minute of blessed relief
Lovers used to show me what i could see
Can't see passed my disbelief
I've got nothing to push me passed my misbelief
A whole lot of nothing nothing inside nothing underneath

My mind's a blank
Totally clean slate
Sinking? I've sank
Feeling like a fake

Getting nowhere
Traffic jams find me
Bitter? Don't care
Shoot me in my sleep

Sadness taught my spoons to bend
Hate to see the end of the day
Nights've got my wounds to mend
Speechless when I intend to say
I need to learn to love again
I need to learn to love again
I need to learn to find the end
And begin again

Take the knife out
Best to leave it in
Hurting? Warns me
It hurts to love again

The Ragman

Because he writes trying to define
Where he was in space and in time
People they think he's depressed
Because he pens thoughts unkind

When he swims in the flowing river
Or falters or stops or laughs and shivers
When he's full of happiness
They kidnap life and try to define her

The sky is falling Chicken Little was right
It's a lot more than the falling of night
Apocalypse and it seems the only thing to know
Is that little chicken yapping "I told you so"

He looks at the Colosseum from atop a hill
It's the last time and that brings him a chill
It's night and gray clouds swim on by
He doesn't run for he has time to kill

The street is hot and his feet are clay
He wonders if he writes what he means to say
Or if time will kill what he says he wants to write
Before Chicken Little steals this fine today

The sky is falling Chicken Little was right
It's a lot more than the falling of night
Apocalypse and it seems the only thing to know
Is that little chicken yapping "I told you so"

From Athené then I must go
No love from 'lita do I show
I have to stop listening to anyone's
Chorus'd lies that might be thrown

No more will fear wet my brow
Or fright at what the night might allow

I'll pick the scraps of love and sorrow
And into the earth will they be sown

To grow under rains of
Clouds of thoughts to know
To live under nights
Under the whispering snows

Rape

Scratch my back—then tear out my eyes
Talon's searching out my cries
Steal my tears—take away my feelings
Give me only pain with no meaning

A pain so searing
Retreating into dark corners
Arrow headed pain
Nothing left clean

Twisting your knife in—rearranging the gag
Pushing me among your dirty rags
Throwing me down—crashing garbage can cymbals
Greasy fingers all but smearing

After you have twisted your knife in
For the last time
Leave me alone—leave me alone
I'll be fine

Scratch my back—then tear out my eyes
Your talons searching out my lies
Steal my tears—take away my feelings
Give me only pain with no meaning

A pain so hollow
Following into dark corners
Time will never tame
Nothing to believe

Leave me alone—leave me alone
I'll be fine

Rewind (Waste Of Rhyme)

(With some alternative lines for added wrinkles in the slinky silky break)

(Girl:)
broke my heart in two
i'm through with you
and i'm glad not so sad
cause you were a waste of time

could write a book 'bout you boy so many ways to describe how you
suck at joy how you you you couldn't even find my toy let alone play well
with others or play in my sandbox thanks a whole helluva lot it was a
lost weekend month and a day and i had to send you packing yesterday
for all that you were lacking not even tracking on my gps nevertheless
you broke my heart in two and now that we're done and through can you
send me the receipt so i can get a refund and hit the delete and get you
out of my life out of my mind out out out out damn spot hit the rewind

(Boy:)
yo yo yo rewind
play back your mind
when you were mine
i made you shine

under your thunder
melted like butter
shock awe 'n' wonder
heart all aflutter

(Girl:)
broke my heart in two
i'm through with you
won't name your name
don't want to waste a rhyme

(Slinky silky break)

it's a crime to waste a rhyme on a fool like you

a tool so cruel i pity the girl who'll take a whirl with you

[alt. lines: so cool so cruel /
/i pity the girl who'll give the world to you
/i pity the girl who thinks the world of you
/i pity the girl who learns from the school of you
/i pity the girl who screws the tool of you]

nothing true through and through I'm so through w you
waste of time gotta rewind before there was you

you were a cheapskate loser a boozer undecided chooser couldn't read
the news or read my lips trash talking shit flash no smoking wit lovers
hah under the covers wanna winning big wanna winning first start at
the finish finish finish take this dish and finish what you came for honey
don't skip the dessert tray no way stay there longer with the cherry on
top blew all my money to smoke yourself to heaven get your damn own
self to eleven elevate yourself elevator going up up up and outta here
out of my life out of my mind out out out out damn spot hit the rewind

(Boy:)
rewind your desire
you lit the fire
climbing the wire
higher and higher

your love was so fine
your lips melted mine
you're so out of line
i wasted your time?

(The thick paste of words up there in those two stanzas are attempted
rap vocals, just in case you were wondering where the line breaks broke
rank and went clubbing on their own.)

Remotely Unseen

My life is conveniently
Divorced into years
These excursions yearly
Usually end with fears

I try to keep to myself
Locking up all my tears
In the safety of my room
Where myself is ever clear

These years divide into weeks
Weeks unfold days
Sometimes outside finds a leak
And sorrow pays

I know life's gonna end
I think I'm living
I know my life maybe later
Will be better
I know what promises to tend
To give away
And the others that need erasure

I know I'm a burden
Not working my share
Really just hurting
Defunding medicare

My life is conveniently
Divorced into years
These excursions yearly
Usually end in tears

I try to keep to myself
Sheltering all my tears
Into the safety of my room
Where myself is ever near

Riding The Bad News Through

(Music by China Moses & Raphaël Lemonnier / Lyrics by China Moses & David Greenberg)

When push comes to shove
And there ain't nowhere to run
No need to go and jump your guns or
Hide your sorrows down in some rum
Sometimes there ain't nothing you can do
Gotta ride the bad news through

Feel like you wanna hide away
Lay low 'til moonlight comes
Maybe change your address and your name
Sneak out the back and be gone
Sometimes there ain't nothing you can do
You gotta ride the bad news through

Forget how you fell for it took hell for it and
If you can't learn to live with it
Let go don't be a fool and dwell on it just level it
'cos you're nothing if you stay with it
Hard but true

Your heart's in lost and found
No one but you around
Not easy to stand your ground when your life is breaking on down
Sometimes there ain't nothing left to do
But ride that bad news through

Forget how you fell for it took hell for it and
If you can't learn to live with it
Let go don't be a fool and dwell on it just level it
'cos you're nothing if you stay with it
Hard but true

Your heart's in lost and found
No one but you around
Not easy to stand your ground when your life is breaking on down

Sometimes somedays the only thing to do
Is ride that bad news through

You gotta do what's right for you
Don't fight it
Realize it
Hold on tight
Sometimes bottom of the bottle is the sweetest
Naked truths are the meanest
You know the song
You know you're strong
Just let it go
Lay low 'n take your pride for a ride
Brace yourself 'n face the tide
You've got nothing left to lose
When you ride the bad news through
Sometimes it's the only thing to do

When push comes to shove
And there ain't nowhere to run

―――――――――

At the time of this collaboration, China Moses was a Paris-based Rough Soul singer, as she described herself, who also happened to present for MTV France. Right now, she's based in Brooklyn, touring the world, and you can catch her *Made In China* radio show on TSF Jazz. She has always been the daughter of the iconic Jazz vocalist Dee Dee Bridgewater. In my former life, at that music agency whose name we will still not be uttering here, we represented Dee Dee. As I covered our social media and anything else marketing and promotion-related, I noticed China tweeting about touring with her Mom. Then, China was tweeting about recording and needing some lyrics. I quickly, immediately, DM'd her and attached some sample lyrics. About a year and a half through back-and-forth messaging and twitterings, we finally collaborated on this song she had already written for her album, *Crazy Blues*. I sent the last revisions off and waited on pins and needles to hear the final mix. *Disparue!* The track never made it onto the album: too rushed, not enough time. China has sung the song live and not to toot my own horn—which, if I could find it, I can't play anyway—but she did write: "The song we wrote together, or should I say, the song he saved me on, is one of my favorite songs to sing." You might have read that on the "Words Blurbed" page under another great quote, the one from Dee Dee. That's two toots, I know. One of these days, I have to make it over there, wherever "there" it is in the world she is touring at the time, and hear this one live.

Road Kill

dontcha use me like it's funny
dontcha make me drive too far
dontcha wanna make it with me, well
dontcha ever piss me off
'cos if you do make your life a freaking hell

lay down turn around kiss the freaking tar
better bet my brakes'll break real hard
or you'll turn out to be road kill

you'll never get nuthin better yet
you'll never get nuthin at all
you'll be one sorry mutt if you
ever find a way to piss me off
when you do better watch your butt

lay down turn around kiss the freaking tar
better bet my brakes'll break real hard
or you'll turn out to be road kill

During my tenure at Rykodisc, among a few hundred other responsibilities, producer and label manager of the HiFi label was one of them. Under that logo and moniker we first reissued a series of albums by the seminal exotica icon of the 1950s and 1960s, and initial HiFi artist, vibraphonist Arthur Lyman (*Taboo!*, *Leis of Jazz*, *Hawaiian Sunset*). We latched onto the retro-sound/lounge/cocktail/tlkl craze of the 1980s with even more HiFi albums. Those CDs out in the marketplace connected me with some incredibly cool nuevo-retro surf bands; one was the all-female Neptunas out of El-Ay. Pamita Neptune told me she was creating another all-girl band, this one playing a hot rod kind of supercharged turbo rock whose members would unfurl supreme car-bitch attitude. Picturing a team of nasty biker chicks decked out in form-fitting leather, though, behind steering wheels of throaty high-performance muscle cars out-running the CHPs on the highways of Cali, I wrote this here "Road Kill." I think I gave them more "violence" than "attitude." Hell, I know I did. Just look at how I make them treat their insignificant others. Which could be why I never heard from Ms. Neptune again. Recently on Facebook, I found Pamita still over there in Cali, but now conjuring spells and selling potions at Madame Pamita's Parlour of Wonders.

Sad Café

Sitting at the Sad Café with a smile cracking
Sitting at the Sad Café me and the waiters laughing
Sitting at the Sad Café reading funny pages
Sitting at the Sad Café staring at the drifters

Looking so stunned

With faces longer than a winter's night
Wasting time ordering up sadness
And misery a miser's tea
For dessert at the Sad Café
At the Sad Café
At the Sad Café
So sad at the Sad Café

(Laugh-it-up solos: I'm not laughing with you
I am laughing at you says the guitar. You're a riot says the drums.
While the bass guitar just hums in the background not really listening,
making up his own jokes, as usual.)

Sitting at the Sad Café cracking a coupla jokes
Sitting at the Sad Café can't stand broken hopes
Have to leave Sad Café laughing at the customers
Who've come to remember there's no starting over

Wait till the check comes

With melodramas longer than their faces
Sad endings are just beginnings
And misery a miser's tea
For dessert at the Sad Café
At the Sad Café
At the Sad Café
So sad at the Sad Café

Scratch That 7yr Itch

Why'd you promise for better or worse
If you'd treat it like some awful curse
Happy or not through thick and thin
Button up your lip or take it on the chin

Just that 7yr itch
When your love irritates
Just that 7yr itch
When your hate penetrates
Just one little catch
Gotta start from scratch

Layers and layers of soap opera sentiment
You think it's rich it's only sediment
Throw away lines find a ditch
Only one thing'll remove this itch

Just that 7yr itch
When your love irritates
Just that 7yr itch
When your hate penetrates
Just one little catch
Gotta start from scratch

See You

I just wanted wanted to see you tonight
I just wanted wanted everything to be right
I should have listened to your premonitions
That you told me over the phone
One of which was to stay safe at home

But I could see you
Could see you loving me today
I could see you
I'm gonna believe it's you when you say

Yes it's you I can tell by the seat
Of your pants and the taste of sweet
Orange lips tongues twisted by taste
Of kisses that--you--paste
On sweet lips quickly as if in haste

I could see you
Could see you
I could see you
Yes I could see you

I found a place you wouldn't believe
Better than the movies besides it's free
Silently the moon spotlights the scene
In rolls a cloud the fog caresses our whispers
Cinema verité it looks more like a dream
But as you said it comes off more like a disaster

It starts to rain as you start to complain
That the leaves have messed up your better dress
And the contacts you lost you want me to pay the cost
We can't go and dance it seems I've lost my pants

I could see you
Could see you
I could see you

Yes I could see you

I just wanted wanted to see you tonight
I just wanted wanted everything to be right
I should have listened to your premonitions
That you told me over the phone
One of which was to stay safe
Stay at home

I could see you
Could see you
I could see you
Yes I could see you

Doo-wop daydreams of a High School date somewhere suburban, in some other
era, for someone else.

Sending Out Signals

(Chorus:)
Sending out signals
A dit-dit-dit ending with a dot
Sending out signals
I thought I said that I love you a lot
Sending out signals
I really said you fire the first shot
Here come the planes

Wartime so hard to keep neutral
Family outings ready shoot to kill
I'm in my basement signaling to you
On my shortwave signaling to you
Sending out signals
Sending out signals
Sending out signals

(Chorus)

Didn't want to be over heard
Trying to spare every word
Never expected the underground
Listening to my shortwave sound
Listening and waiting
And ready and ready
And ready to pounce

(Chorus)

Sexting

twitter facebook snapchat foursquare instagram
who's got the time really who gives a damn
tweeting texting selfies sharing's so banal
hand me some jameson and a fine looking gal

i get so wrapped up in this message of the medium
hours upon hours getting lost in the tedium
going facebooking with my few thousand friends
my status beats their status to the bitter end

don't need don't want no social media
socialize socialize please talk to me please
fine hips fine lips that's my criteria
socialize socialize go on be a tease
come here babe let my fingers be your man
socialize socialize need the human touch
snapchat that sexting? no i need it on my...instagram

(Bridge)
want my music in my face and not up on the cloud
want my girl in my lap and not out on the prowl
an s.m.s. is an s.o.s. that you don't have a life
keep on texting guys i'll be at home with your wife
i know things i learned in books make her jump and shout
stay up late jive talking i'll know her inside and out
just one night i'll show her what she has been missing
shut the door and we'll put the sex back into sexting

twitter facebook snapchat foursquare instagram
who's got the time really who gives a damn
tweeting texting selfies sharing's so banal
hand me some jameson and a fine looking gal

i get so wrapped up in this message of the medium
hours upon hours getting lost in the tedium
going facebooking with my few thousand friends
my status needs to beats their status to the bitter end

don't need don't want no social media
socialize socialize please talk to me please
fine hips fine lips that's my criteria
socialize socialize go on be a tease
come here babe got your number
socialize socialize need the human touch
photoshopped for my tumblr

don't need don't want no social media
socialize socialize please talk to me please
fine hips fine lips that's my criteria
socialize socialize go on be a tease
come here babe let my fingers be your man
socialize socialize need the human touch
snapchat that sexting? no i need it on my...instagram

She Still Says No!

There's a pain
A pain in my heart
How does
How does love start
I was strong
Now I'm falling apart
I can't find the words to say
Please don't leave me please stay
She's got me down on my knees
She's tired of my begging her please
She still says no

She says no
And mind no never mind
She can't see
Can't see my love is blind
I'm insane
I'm going out of my mind
She's an angel a halo of light
I dream about her every night
She's the only girl in my dreams
I get to write and direct her scenes
She still says no

My heart is stung by needles and pins
And my love has nothing to say
Blind love leads my blind ambition
And Justice looks the other way
She still says no

She says no
There's a pain in my heart
She can't see
Can't see my love is blind
She says no
How does love start
She can't see
I'm going out of my mind

Shooby Dooby Moon

Shooby Dooby Shooby Dooby Moon
Shooby Dooby Shooby Dooby Moon / I'm afraid of you

Read enough books on romance
Nothin' on how to cope with cramps
Or be romantic unzipping pants
Or using your tongue not licking stamps
Under the Shooby Dooby Shooby Dooby Moon

Shooby Dooby Shooby Dooby Moon
Shooby Dooby Shooby Dooby Moon / I'm afraid of you

This year I'm a gonna graduate
This year I gotta get a date
I've love love enough for eight
Eight's enough enough to fornicate
Under the Shooby Dooby Shooby Dooby Moon

Shooby Dooby Shooby Dooby
Shooby Dooby Shooby Dooby
Shooby Dooby Shooby Dooby Moon / I'm afraid of you

Eight's enough but I don't have one
Doctor Doctor prescibe me a potion
That'll leave bra elastic smoking
Under this Shooby Dooby
Shooby Dooby
Sh-Sh-Sh-ooby Shooby Dooby Shooby Dooby Moon

Shooby Dooby Moon was a funny, hilarious, 1950s-themed alien invasion movie
script written by George A. Romero. Yes, George A. Romero of *Creepshow* and
the *Living Dead* flicks. I had to be involved somehow just hearing about the
script, so I wrote this lyrical ditty as the perfect theme song for the flick if it ever
got made.

Romero wrote this in the 1980s, way before CGI was remotely realistic. The plot
centered around amorous aliens landing in suburbia U.S.A. circa the 1950s. If

the filmmakers were going to shoot anything halfway decent with the critters kinda looking alienish and alive, not cartoony, and seamlessly interacting with people—they needed a good amount of cash to robotize them or produce some costly frame-by-frame special effects animating finely detailed models.

The producers could never cut the SFX budget down where they could have the aliens acting and looking like believable beings and still retain a good wad of decent money to make the film as well as release it and have some left over to pay their overhead, alimony, second mortgages. The flick never got made, and I never got to pitch the song through my friends working with the production team. *Shooby Dooby Moon* would have been a hilarious film with the aliens sex-crazed and running around Middle America aching for a bit of action with those 1950s film clichés: the overly pretty, unnaturally buxom and buoyant Cheerleaders.

A George A. Romero comedy! Imagine the memes!

Romero's production team saw this as a mainstream success, but I understood the film had all the makings of an excellent underground hit. Most assuredly, with George at the helm, an enduring cult favorite. Maybe the Studios understood that as well. Cult films don't usually make the big money needed to pay for the initial production, the next layer of expensive special effects, then post, prints, marketing, and don't forget the red carpet partying for all the cast, crew, press, executives, and better halfs, or their girlfriends, while also returning an enormous profit handing the Suits a sizable bonus at year's end.

In my fantasy version of an alternative reality (where my manic dreams of success sometimes frolic to this day), the film exists. It plays midnights at all the hip theatres still left in business. And that film opens with a killer theme song setting the perfect tone of 1950s High School horny. And that song, which is this song, has become a cult fave as well, and at many ComicCons for decades afterward, I get to sign and sell exorbitantly-priced copies of the 45 rpm single and hang with the, by then, ultra-famous stars of the film.

The single's B-side? "Dream On," of course.

Silent Night

Can you feel me can you hold me tight inside
Can you squeeze me don't release me squirming to hide
Can you feel me can you hold me tight inside
Can you squeeze me don't release me squirming to hide

Those magic fingers caress my brain
Hold me a little close just the same
It's these moments give me such a rush
Tears from my eyes cause you to crush

Can you feel me can you see me squirming to hide
It's up to you thoughts of what to do coughing to cry
Can you feel me can you wind me tight inside
Can you squeeze me don't release me squirming to hide

Can you cassette me please
Bundle me up to my knees
Brown paper bag it
Wait a minute hold my nose I'm gonna sneeze

Can you feel me can you hold me tight inside
Can you squeeze me don't release me squirming to hide
Can you bind me
Can you find me
Can you feel me
Can you hold me
Just once more
Tight inside

Sky Babies

Am I just imagining
Or is that girl out of tune
Out of wack
Out of sync
Predicting a new doom

Or am I remembering
An old forgotten message
A déjà vu
The last rerun
From my out-dated heritage

Somehow it all seems familiar
Someday they're gonna rob your store and kill ya

Babies of the Sky
Never left us alone
Babies of the sky
Sky Babies are made of stone

The fathers sit on their lawn chairs finishing their beers
And sitting next to them sitting near
Are their over and under umbilical brides
Talking about their intestinal prides

Sky Babies are dropping
Into the house
SkyBabies are coming
From the chimney into the bed
SkyBabies just pretending
Lying over and playing dead

They can't fool me
I can see through their formula lie
They aren't even born yet
So how can they sit and cry

Sky Babies are dropping
Out of the ground into the sky
Sky Babies just pretending
To look like you and I

The fathers with their
Bellies full of beer
Want their wives to father their sons

And be a mirror image
A mirrored image of them
With the mirror tilted
And carnival flavored
With the clouds and sunrises painted in

Am I just pretending
Or is that chick out of tune
Out of line
Out of sync
Predicting the old doom

Or am I just dreaming
An old forgotten message
A déjà vu
The last rerun
Of my over-rated heritage

Somehow it all seems familiar
Sky Babies gonna rob your store and kill ya

Sleep Tight

Dealing with demons
Wrestling with fantasies
Crawling with desires
When all you desire is a good night's serenity

Sleep tight—nothing is what it seems
Sleep tight—don't even dare to dream
Sleep tight—can't get it out of your head
Sleep tight—what's that under your bed

No one can help you
Even if you try to scream
It's no one's business
More or less you're on your own in your dreams

Sleep tight—all alone in the night
Sleep tight—don't let the bed bugs bite
Sleep tight—is something in the bed
Sleep tight—crawling up to your head

Mashing with monsters
Excites your curiosity
It also killed the cat
Remember that when you can't fall back asleep

Sleep tight—nothing is what it seems
Sleep tight—don't even dare to dream
Sleep tight—can't get it out of your head
Sleep tight—what's that under your bed

Sneaker Love

Sneaker, Sneaker, Sneaker Love
Sneaker, Sneaker, oh my Sneaker Love

I don't have my thoughts down right
Cause I haven't been waiting up nights
Worrying about my
Sneaker, Sneaker, Sneaker Love
Sneaker, Sneaker, Sneaker Love

Oh my Sneaker Love

All this talk and doing nothing
Let's get down to doing something
Holding hands in the park
It's my feeling of being amazed
And my feeling of being with you
Has left me a little crazed

It's the glamour of the fifty-mile cut down to size
We can do it in a while just have to economize
Don't tell me you have to walk when you can run
Once you start gotta finish what you've begun

Sneaker, Sneaker, Sneaker Love
Sneaker, Sneaker, oh my Sneaker Love

I don't have my thoughts down right
Cause I haven't been waiting up nights
Worrying about my
Sneaker, Sneaker, Sneaker Love
Sneaker, Sneaker, Sneaker Love

Oh my Sneaker
Oh my Sneaker
Oh my Sneaker
Love

Something For Nothing

Somebody's doing nothing
Nothing's being done
Okay for some not for me

You see I need love and love's not free
Love's never come running to me
Bought maps and charts and watched TeeVee
Love's never where it's supposed to be

Somebody's doing nothing
Nothing's being done
Okay for some not for me

You see when I rest I try dreams
To find new ways and means
All this talk of love's simple schemes
I rip apart to find the seams

Somebody's doin...
(The nuthin' doin' solos here...or maybe here.)

Do nothing sit still be quiet
I'm no kid anymore
Do nothing sit still be quiet
I'm no kid anymore
Doing nothing doing nothing
Doing nothing makes me tired
And I'm tired of sleeping alone

Somebody's doing nothing
Nothing's being done
Swell for some not for me

Absolutely nothing's being done
An empty life is the prize you've won
A wonderful prize all your own
Oh my how well we've grown

Somebody's doing nothing
Nothing's being done
Fine for some not for me

You see I need love and love's not free
Love's never come running to me
Bought maps and charts and watched TeeVee
Love's never where it's supposed to be
Love's never where it's supposed to be
Love's never where it's supposed to be

Love is never where it is supposed to be

So Much Better Than That

(big bass groove for the open)

Cocaine eyes and satin alibis
Streaks of jealousy just can't let it be
Sex without love slap comes to shove
Sex in the air is like you don't care
Physical threats and love (pause) love without sex
I'm better than that

If you want me you'll have to do better than that
If you need me you'll have to be better than that
Much better than that

Listen up kid all for a laugh now seriously
It's not games night no damn winner seriously
Seriously love

You're my sinner goddamn hero you hurt me so
Lackadaisical two-faced liar burned me so

Was a third degree

Better than that is where I'm at
Don't take me for granted
Better than that is where I'm at
You're all I wanted
Better than that is where I'm at
Don't need anymore pity
Better than that is where I'm at
Stop this feeling shitty

[late night antics break—rip apart old + new songs to answer the dudes
back]

Drink your night out with the boys (so much better than that)
Playing with your own toys (so much better than that)
Way down inside you think I need (so much better than that)

Under your thumb is where I bleed (so much better than that)
Sucking face with the groupies (so much better than that)
Lovering me when you're loopy (so much better than that)
Talk talk talking about Xboxes (so much better than that)
On & on about Megan Foxe's (so much better than that)
[etc.]

Comme ci comme ca is where you are
Go on without me you'll go far
In the gutter and the sewer feathered and tarred
Got the best of me don't take the rest of me
I'm better than that

If you want me you'll have to do better than that
If you need me you'll have to be better than that

Much better than that

Listen up kid all for a laugh now seriously
It's not games night no damn winner seriously

Seriously love

You're my sinner goddamn hero you hurt me so
Lackadaisical two-faced liar you burned me so

Was a third degree

Better than that is where I'm at
Don't take me for granted
Better than that is where I'm at
You're all I wanted
Better than that is where I'm at
Don't need anymore pity
Better than that is where I'm at
Stop this feeling shitty

Sour Lime

(Traditional, lyrics by Jonathan Levey and David Greenberg)

Let me tell you man about the sour lime
You take a bite and it's mighty fine
But don't get fooled by its tangy taste
Just throw it away 'cause it ain't no waste

(Chorus:)
Sour lime / Sour lime / Sour lime
If you eat too much you won't go dancing
You won't feel like romancing
You'll lose your woman to someone else

The tides come in
The tides go out
The days can be bitter
If you pass the time
Eating sour lime

(Repeat chorus and go and jam some real dance-inducing reggae and
add the traditional chorus when appropriate)

(Traditional chorus:)
Don't you touch that thing
Your mama's gonna know
If you touch that thing
Your mama's gonna know (How?)
If you touch that thing
Your belly's gonna show

———————

A "found" lyric from 1977, during a stint of undergraduate anthropology spent
on Cat Island, the Bahamas. A group of us, ten Ithaca College students, traveled

down there with our professor, Dr. Joel Savishinsky, to learn about the Cat Islanders: their history, present relationships, culture, entanglements, politics, and, of course, about ourselves.

It was actual fieldwork, mind you, not at all like the beach holiday our friends back at school dreamed up for us. In fact, we completed a hefty book from all the writings, published as *Strangers No More*, as well as presented papers at an anthropology conference in 1978.

On the Island, in the evenings, after group discussions and writing in our journals, we usually drifted out to the bar in front of our house to soak up the nighttime culture while downing drinks with the islanders. Some nights, it got very, shall we say, "lively"; more like cultural submersion than observation. More like the college students we were than the Cultural Anthropologists we had yet to become.

Rendered here is our version of the traditional song Jon Levey and I "learned" on one of those nights. Most assuredly, this is not genuinely 100 percent traditional since we "recreated" it after soaking up one too many Dark 'n' Stormies and beers to wash down the very spicy "Sous" (Goat's Head Soup) with words we thought we heard.

Unlike the Stones' album cover, this version of Sous had no skull poking out, and probably no head was ever near, let alone immersed in the pot. Instead, heaped with lots of goat bits and bobs and bones and was spiced up hotter than usual. We later assumed it was so the American Student Anthropologists in the crowd could buy out the bar's stash of ice-cold liquid refreshments.

Springtime In December

Springtime in December could be July
It's time to remember you can reply
It's warmer than it's been in years
Must be the climate change most of us fear
Go and deny it
Rubbish science
There's no why of it
Springtime in December nearly July

Springtime in December maybe July
If you can forgive me so can I
You are the reason I persevere
I'll hang my head if you can pull near
Oh the thrill of it
Smug in defiance
Heats up the chill of it
Springtime in December who needs July

Springtime in December nearly July
It's time to remember you can reply
It's warmer than it's been in years
Must be the climate change most of us fear
Go and deny it
Rubbish science
There's no why of it
Springtime in December could be July

Stardance

I'm wearing mirrored glasses over my faceless beauty
You can't see my eyes or savor my ecstasy

I'm here behind my mike searching all around
Playing what we hope you like yet you all act like clowns

I know we're not Elton John you're not Coney Island Baby
We're the snakes of Alice and you're his SkyBabies

I know what it is you're seeking
I know how you think you're failing
Just give me one more chance
Take my hand and we'll Stardance

I'll put sparkle on my eyes so we can Stardance
We'll bullet to the skies so we can Stardance

Clip on your jets of neon and Top Ten hits
We'll murder Elton John with thundering bliss

I know what it is you're seeking
I know how you think you're failing
Just give me one more chance
Take my hand and we'll Stardance

If you date-check the references, you'll find I wrote this a long, long time ago, around the era when the glamsters and their music used to make me smile and want to emulate the songs of Lou and Alice and The New York Dolls within my lyrics. Not the dress, god no. I topple over in heels, and eyeliner makes my eyes tear up in a weird way. Could it be that an update is needed for this one? Or perhaps some band, like Foster The People, should leave it as it is to inject the high dose of retro irony, the metaphorical adrenaline if you must, needed to re-animate the life of these lyricals? Yes! And stat!

The Stars Smile The Wind Laughs

The stars above
And the lights far away flicker
The wind blows
Its cold breath washing upon my face
My eyes wander
And somehow my thoughts give unto laughter

Because

My Janus
Both his heads looked toward the past
He saw Winter
But couldn't unlock the door to Spring
He dwelled
On the cold and ice he hoped wouldn't last
He couldn't see
What life the Spring would bring

I haven't been ready for the present
Because I've been sleeping in the past
I had no time for the future
And I had thought of my friends last

Now that I've been awakened
By this strange and different night
I've made no map for my walking
Just guided by the smiling jewels of light

The wind blows
Its cold breath washing upon my face
I feel more than alive
In trying to savor every taste

The stars smile
And the wind laughs through the night
Full of that joy
That will scare away the fright

The stars smile
And the wind laughs
And the night sparkles
Feeling more than alive

The stars smile
And the wind laughs Blowing through the night
Feeling more than alive

The stars smile
And the wind laughs through the night
Full of that joy
That should scare away the fright

Now that I've been awakened
By this strange and different night
I've made no plans for my tomorrows
Just guided by the smiling jewels of light

The wind blows
Its cold breath washing upon my face
I feel more than alive
In trying to savor every taste

The stars smile
And the wind laughs through the night
Full of that joy
Please oh please scare away the fright

Strange Agents On The Assembly Line

When Susan pointed them out to me
She called them the strange agents of jealousy
I called them the murderers of happenstance
I guess mystery means a little more to me

Strange Agents
Talking up their sleeves checking ear plugs
Strange Agents
Making us believe we're all bugged
Strange Agents
We're on teevee on the elevator
Strange Agents
Even bugged Sue's D.C. vibrator
Oh so Strange Agents

I couldn't quite see through the haze and dust
Almost couldn't hear Muzak® playing "Diamonds & Rust"
I saw 'em standing over by the drill press
They were so bored they wanted to have cared less
I saw them talking with hands in pants
Looking at Sue and me behind silvry Foster Grants®

Strange Agents
Talking up their sleeves checking ear plugs
Strange Agents
Making us believe we're all bugged
Strange Agents
We're on teevee on the elevator
Strange Agents
Even bugged Sue's D.C. vibrator
Oh so Strange Agents

I couldn't even start to turn night into day
Almost couldn't hear Muzak® playing "Purple Haze"
I saw 'em standing over by my drill press
If we were sober we could've cared less

Strange Agents
Talking up their sleeves checking ear plugs
Strange Agents
Making us believe we're all bugged
Strange Agents
We're on teevee on the elevator
Strange Agents
Eventually used Sue's D.C. vibrator
Oh so Strange Agents

Strangers No More

Some things change
Some things never do
Strange as it seems
We're strangers no more

Plastic flamingos on the lawn (by the pool)
Beads of chlorine in your hair
There's a coldness in your hands
And in the love we try to share

Some things change
Some things never do
Strange as it seems
(No singing over melody)

The sun burns orange yellow
Through the selfish shade trees
And you're sore and jealous
At Hencil's party in the country

Some things change
Some things never do
Strange as it seems
(   )

When you wake up in the morning
You draw the shades down
The sun you keep detouring
From ever coming to town

Some things change
Some things never do
Strange as it seems
(   )

When you wake up in the morning
I can tell by your eyes

The dreams that you've dreamed
And the troubles that you'll realize

Some things change
Some things never do
Strange as it seems
We're strangers no more

Stuck In Reverse

Drive me hard
Drive me slow
Take me where
You want to go

But don't change gears on me
Or you'll be stuck in reverse
Going down hills about one fifty three
In the baddest ass hearse you'll ever see

By the light of the moon
By the glare of the sun
Keep it tender
Keep it fun

Don'tcha change gears on me
Or you'll be stuck in reverse
Ramming your 'vette into a tree
Say good night and good luck nurse

Down the boulevard
And on to Oxnard
I'll take you there
Truth or dare

But don't change gears on me
Or you'll be stuck in reverse
Right through the blackest
Black hole of the bitchin' universe

Heat me up
Cool me down
Take me all around
This freakazoid town

But don't change gears on me
Or you'll be stuck in reverse

Stuck in reverse
Stuck in reverse
Stuck in reverse
Stuck stuck
Stuck in reverse

Get your ass outta here
Bye-bye babe

I got what you want
If that's what you need
Don't you dare hurt me
You'll damn well bleed

I got what you want
If that's what you need
The best you'll ever have
Nothing better'n me

Change your gears on me
You'll be squealing in reverse
You'll be squealing in reverse
You'll be squealing in reverse
You'll be squealing in reverse
You'll be squealing in reverse
Got it?

One more dragster-chick lyrical written for, and never sung by, the proposed hot-rod version of Pamita's Neptunas. Fumes of lyrical inspiration mainly came from hours and hours spent making the Big Daddy Roth Rat Fink model cars back in my geeky youth. I'm sure all the vapors of airplane glue I inhaled didded my brainwave functions during those long nights assembling the models and helped to implant these fantasies, the unstable characters, brutish imagery, and the song's base attitude. Or is that a rationalization to explain away the punk violence? Though, this would have been a great title sequence theme for one of those American International Picture Biker Movies Tarintino loves; *The Hard Ride*, *Angel Unchained*, and the like. Perhaps the scripters of those flicks were flying high on Duco Cement as well?

Suddenly

suddenly
falling like a ton of bricks
suddenly
had your fill of my kicks
suddenly
not your only desire
suddenly
honey baby you are such a liar

suddenly suddenly
suddenly free

you said what you wanted was honesty
honestly you never knew what you wanted
one minute up and up the next crashing down
meltdown with rumors burning up in my head

suddenly
i say all the wrong words
suddenly
you know what i deserve
suddenly
jokes are now barbed-wired
suddenly
honey baby you are such a liar

suddenly suddenly
suddenly free

moods so dark and depressingly thick
what a trick to find love when your love was on fire
taking me to heaven though the gates of hell
you showed me well was where you found desire

suddenly
you want to cut me out
suddenly

doing the scream and shout
suddenly
everything is deja-vu
suddenly
honey baby so through with you

suddenly suddenly
suddenly free

You know the type. In a perpetual swoon, undying love, lasting, she says, like,
you know, forever. Pledges it's the truth more than a few times, late at night,
from the other side of the bed, excitingly whispered in the dark. Then dumps you.
Then she writes a top-ten song about her heartbreak, and another. More than a
few times. This is not her song. This is your song.

Sunglasses for Peter: The Installation Party

Words come to mind
Then they blow themselves away
Names start to fade
As the faces begin to say

You know who I am / You know me
Do you know who I am do you know me

A blankness starts
Making me stare straight ahead
I feel embarrassed
I wish I were dead

I wish I weren't scared
To say Hello to their Goodbyes
To keep their names
Catalogued in my mind

Do you know me / Do you know who I am
Do you remember do you know who I am

Who am I / Do I belong here
Who are you / Don't you understand

I feel like it's opening night
For a retro of Picasso
Where no one says hello
From New York to Toronto
And those Vassar Dreams
Could be Andy Warhol Queens

Who am I / Do you know who I am
Who am I / Do you know who I am / Who am I

They need directions
Towards their stand-in recognition
And nothing could be better

Than playing stock in the News Theatre

Do you know me / Kiss me quick before they see
Do you know me / Do you know who I am
Who am I / Do I belong here
Do you know me / Kiss me quick make it real
Before they see what they believe

Words come to mind
Then they blow themselves away
Names start to fade
As the faces begin to say

You know who I am
You know me
Do you know who I am do you know me

No one ever says hello
From New York to Buffalo
All those Barnard Gals
Could be Andy Warhol Pals (y'know what I mean?)
And when Bowie stops predicting doom
Then end will be all the more soon
'Cause nobody knows who they are
And the faces ask from their cars

Who am I
Do you know who I am
Do you know me
Go take a guess
Do you know me
Do you know who I am
Do I belong here
My life is such a mess
Do you know me
Do you know who I am

(Slow fade out ending just before the dude wakes up to the real world)

The Sun Glides

I saved the morning before sunrise
For the girl who hates her name
But her newspaper held lies
And for her love was too much to blame

Someday she'll make it oh yes
It's not too hard to fry eggs is it?
I think I'm right unless
My mind has lost the cause to wit

The sun glides / The days hold long shadows
The wind whips / Its cold at all my isolation allows
The cool night / Is Bible leather bound
Here she comes / A long cool woman whose echo is no sound

(Chorus:)
I've got a long cool woman along because
I've got a long cool woman along because
I've got a long cool woman along because
I'm in love with her / I'm in love

(Background chorus of skeptical babes who don't believe in love:)
Is that any reason?

Watching the day burning
Afloat on a wild stream
Watching the day turning
Around and around and

Around she goes spinning tales
From her shimmering dreams
Her voice a nightingale
Floats on air that sheens

(Chorus and repeat chorus through the sheeny fade out)

(Sheeny skeptical babes repeat as well)

Supposin' To Be A Constitution
(Protest Song Nr. 12)

Little Bobby ain't on the pavement no more
He's behind his processed walnut door
And were not in the basement no more
Stockpiling our medicine store
We're supposed to be grown up now
Bobbie's recording telling us how
But he knows we don't need a preacher
Much less a second-rate teacher

We've got to do it on our own learn from our own mistakes
We've got to do it on our own and see what it really takes

We know about the government
And how it's a ship of fools
We've got to go on out on the pavement
And tell them we're not fools—as well
Supposed to be grown up now
Zimmerman's got his great Jesus date
We're trying as hard as we know how
And now they're just making us pay at the gate

We've got to do it on our own learn from our own mistakes
We've got to do it on our own and see what it really takes

The future looks awfully distant
Especially from where I stand
But we can handle resistance
If everybody lends a hand
We're supposed to be grown up now
Why are we still fighting
Talking about a revolution—hey hey
Or drumming up the same old war
We're supposed to be grown up now
Passed the age of shooting
Passed the age of prostitution
And nailing shut our doors

We've got to do it on our own learn from our own mistakes
We've got to do it on our own and see what it really takes

We're supposed to be grown up now
Knowing right and wrong and where to look
No more answers from self-help books
Look into the wind, just look

TeeVee, Dinner, Table, Chair & Stove

I'm taking it slow as I try to
Sneak through the front bay window
I really don't belong here
But I think I'll stay another day although

I think I'm hiding from my love
When I walk out can't stand her shouting
I think I'm hiding from my love
When she kisses me and hugs me then goes off to see
Someone else
But I think I'll stay another day although

My sweet wife Harmony
Is coming at me with a butcher's knife
I don't think she loves me
I think my wife she wants my life

I'm not too sure about Harmony
While she says she loves me she don't know
She also sleeps with Harold
But I think I'll stay another day
I think I'll stay another day
I think I'll stay another day
Cause my wife Harmony knows how to treat me just right
Everything else ain't worth the fight

Talk To Plants

Down Thompson Street
Come the hustlers and penny arcade switchblades
Around where Bleeker
Looks bleak sit the young handsome gays
Eyeing you up and down
What are you worth pound for pound
With the hip trick kids
Prancing and dancing around like they were clowns

Talk to plants
And they'll grow and
Talk to people
And they'll understand

I'm a ticket holder to this Sunday matinee
But not tidy in my orchestra seat watching the play
I can't feel lost in the comfort of a crowd
While the street is in heat yelling much too loud
Instead I've got my box seat in my hotel room
Peering at the performance from my window
I'm dying (spent of life) in this room
Trying to understand who I was and why

Why you felt you couldn't love me
Why it was over and done and dead

Talk to plants
And they'll grow and
Talk to people
And they'll understand

I trundle at nights alone
Trying to sort out my mistakes crying yelling at the phone
Why I did the things you asked of me
Trying to sort out my dreams my memories

A drunk from in front

Of the Other End in exchange for change said to me
Talk to plants and
They'll grown and talk to people and they'll understand
You weren't around
Because you didn't come around to talking to me
And when I asked
It was nothing I could possibly understand

Maybe I wasn't
As strong as you wanted me to be
But if you say
You need someone stronger that's just copping out
Because you're not
Growing up enough to really see
That you're submitting
Yourself to a servant's role and that's just dropping out

Talk to plants
And they'll grow and
Talk to people
And they'll understand

Well I'm not a plant
Because I don't think I grow
And you didn't think I grew
And you didn't think I was human
Because you didn't think I'd understand

Them Track Star Blues

I wanna be a track star
Oooo lace up my Adidas® every night
I wanna be a track star
Oooo lace 'em up real tight

Oh baby don't you start now
I'm gonna race into your heart
I can run the mile 'round you baby
Let me relay and do my part

Oh I wanna be a track star
Don't--let--me--down
Oh I wanna be a track star
I'm getting the track star blues down

Losing you is like
Losing the championship
Losing you is like
Losing my spyayayayayayyyyyyyyyikes
Oh baby I won't get another like you
Oh baby won't get another that I like

Oh I wanna be a track star
I'm gonna win with you
Oh I wanna be a track star
Baby wait till I get a hold on you

(Blues variations of the "I'm a steam roller" variety, baby)

The track is weighing me down
I can feel the pressures right now
The race is nearing the end
And the blues is giving me the bends

Oooo I wanna be a track star

(Etcetera, etcetera, etcetera until it hurts like a charley horse)

These People Here Need You

You'd better watch where it is you walk
Take account of how happy is your talk
These people here are watching you

Don't laugh too loud or smile too often
That small talk or that joke could be a nail in your coffin
These people here are watching you

Painted eyes and questioning mouths
Don't talk with your mouth full it's not polite
These people here are using you
Don't push too hard (OUCH) I'm too tight

The walls of your morals are thin
Once it was a she now it's a him
These people here need you

Ask them who they really are
They'll all promise to make you a star
But you'd better watch where you walk
Take account of how you talk
These people here are watching you

They are people who need you
Yes really really really need you

They Slept In Tents (Old Version)

Jane sleeps intensely intent on sleeping the day away
She calls "Oh my God" although she's rarely brave
Jane must be dreaming as she tosses the night away
She dreams of Tulsa and small Egyptian fools
Of Mobile mechanics and their sweaty tools

She yells through the night:
They slept in tents
As though I should care

But I fear for her fever her forehead is raining
And a mist clouds her eyes and a chill cools the house

I turn to the TeeVee and find there the pyramids of Memphis
And shoppers at the A&P® who push around thoughts of incest
And newscasters sane enough to talk to talking heads
For Cronkite's in En-Why and Reasoner's in DeeCee
And I'm on vacation, call this taking it easy?

Jane quotes through the coughs
They slept with insects
As though they would dare

Jane sleeps intensely intent on sleeping the day away
She calls "Oh Jeffrey" though my name is really Dave
Jane must be dreaming as she tosses the night away
She dreams of Tulsa and small Egyptian fools
Of Mobile mechanics and their sweaty tools

She yells at the night
They slept within sex
As though it were rare

(Note: anyone taking on this song should obviously update the
broadcasters with the latest stars of the world of news—or localize
the lyric to make it a tad more coherent for the average Joe or Jane.
Otherwise it will be just another dusty relic from those sordid '70s.)

They Wonder Why Things Don't Change

Men love women who hurt them
Women love men just because
But when the hurt is real and there's nothing to feel
Is when love seems a lost cause

Men love women who hurt them
Women love men just because
But when the hurt is real and there's nothing to feel
Is when love is a lost cause

Just because you're in love
Just because you're in pain
Doesn't mean that life needs to be insane
When you're down on the floor

Just because love hurts
Just because its love
Don't have 2b beaten down go rise above
Need to choose one way either/or

You wonder why things don't change
Just because
You wonder why things don't change
Just because

Grabbing hold of an eternal flame
Deny the pain live in shame you stay the same you lose your claim you
have to aim
Higher than
Just because

Men love women who hurt them
Women love men just because
But when the hurt is real and there's nothing to feel
Is when love is a lost cause

Just because you're in love

Just because you're in pain
Doesn't mean that life needs to be insane
When you're down on the floor

Just because love hurts
Just because its love
Don't have 2b beaten down go rise above
Need to choose right now more

This lyrical started as a tweet by Sawandi Simon (a Jamaican musician/
producer/great dad and a cohort in the IR::Indigenous Resistance crew, whom
I introduced you to a few dozen of pages back in one of these informational
asides). Sawandi was grousing about those guys who stay in abusive
relationships. I tweeted back a verse and was inspired a few nights later. Of
course, Sawandi wrote back, *dem wonder why 'tings don't change*, but I couldn't
pull that off—no dreads, too white, Jewish, suburban Connecticut. You know,
tennis rackets and all. Though we did have spliffs, calling them doobies before
we found out about Bob Marley. If someone does record this one down in
Kingston town by some miracle of miracles, they can call it just about anything
they want. Because the way Jamaicans say anything in their patois, the English-
based creole, as the linguists define it, will nudge the song closer to the setting
of Sawandi's original complaint.

This Night Wounds Time

I'm waiting impatiently to see you again
Right now all I have is your voice on the telephone
And a photograph that you cared to send
I want to hold you but have no choice 'till you get home

The night wounds my thinly veiled sanity
The dark stabs at my loneliness—time slows down
I want to see you right in front of me
But all around me is darkness to which I'm bound

The rain like tears kisses my wet cheeks
The wind howls through the trees searching for me
The night peels away my vanity
I'm so much alone with only me and nothing to see

This night wounds time
Making it impossible to heal
This night wounds time
Numbing just enough to feel

That I'm cold and wet and I've been crying
How can I forget it's on you that I'm relying
So please don't forget there is no denying

That I'm waiting impatiently to see you again
Right now all I have is your voice on the telephone
And a photograph that you cared to send
I want to hold you but have no choice 'till you get home

Time to dig out your LP of King Crimson's *Starless and Bible Black*. Right, 'cos that was such a massive popular album, I know, and everyone had to have one! Kidding. If you were a fan of Crimson and still have the release where it is handy, take a look-see on the back cover and find the enigmatic phrase "this night wounds time." Those words ping-ponged around in my mind until this little something fell out. While fact-checking this note, I found out the art is a visual quotation from the oeuvre of artist Tom Phillips, also the designer of that Crimson album; one snippet from his "treated Victorian novel" titled, *A Humument*.

Throbbing Funk

Kiss these lips splatter thinking
Kiss these lips jaw some pinking
Kiss these lips tounge 'n' teeth
Kiss these lips and what's beneath

It's a throbbing throbbing funk
Throbbing sobbing robbing bobbing
Throbbing throbbing funk

Suction cups Jabberwockie
Suction cups send me lucky
Suction cups climbing walls
Suction cups suspend and falls

It's a throbbing throbbing funk
Throbbing sobbing robbing bobbing
Throbbing throbbing funk

Too To Do

ooo ooo ooo
i would love to make love to you
you you you
but all you are is sad and blue
blue blue blue
yet all i do is think of you
you you you
deny you ever said you loved me too

too to do
you're a little bit insane
doop de doo
you've got inside my brain
loop de loo
you've shown me the way to blue
too to do
but never how to get to you the truly you

you rile me up and put me down
little lost doll so broken-down
searching for the love you lost
such misery comes at a cost
give me a mirror give me a face
there's so much here i should erase
need you more just because
i'm less the me i thought i was
stay with me all night long
messing with my right and wrong
I've fallen deep in love with you
now i wonder who was

ooo ooo ooo
i would love to make love to you
you you you
but all you are is sad and blue
blue blue blue
yet all i do is think of you

you you you
deny you ever said you loved me too

too to do
you're a little bit insane
doop de doo
you've got inside my brain
loop de loo
you've shown me the way to blue
too to do
but never how to get to you the truly you

Traveled Too Far

Seeing through the reeds
The boats float so effortless
Under seamless skies
Whose unstranded clouds pause to rest
On whispering leaves
Whose secrets old men forget
In beachless beds
And surf white fishing nets
The birds circle
Playing their own little game
Wandering little
I've found I have done the same
Traveled over
All over the world time and again
Looked for joy
Borrowing love from those who lend
In beachless beds
Where love was so effortless

But I've found
My Sherri
But I've found
I've traveled too far for love
Traveled too far
For love

I've traveled in many trains
Slept under the stars in many lands
Slept through many rains
And worked the flesh of my hands
I've found I've gone too far
Seems I shouldn't've left home
The travels been too hard
And too many selfish times spent alone
Playing the wistful man
Just fitting into the hero's pants
Cheap cigarettes and wine

And wasted talk into cheap romance

But I've found
My Sherri
But I've found
I've traveled too far for love
Traveled too far
For love Pretty whisper scenes
I've seen and painted into
Anxious portraits
Of travels of looking for you
Portraits of words
Of travels looking for you
My love

With you here admist the reeds
Silent whispers talk of love with the leaves
Talk of love
That I've found my Sherri
That I've found I've traveled too far for love

True Blue

this is not my happy face
i'm not in my happy place
because of you
yes because of you
it's all you

you don't play well with others
and your jealousy smothers
it's all true
yes it's all true
true blue

you had to win every race
had to put me in my place
all about you
yes all about you
it's all you

wanna rip out your bleeping heart
and baby that's just the start
wanna rip you from limb to limb
hows that for keeping trim
rip off your pants and shirt
wanna kiss you to see you hurt
my love is black and blue
yes my love is black and blue
true blue

got your so-called jollies
with other little dollies
had to choose
you had to choose
now you lose

ego's as big as your head
sorry was never a word you said
all about you

yes all about you
it's all you

don't know what to do
now i'm without you
it's all true
yes it's all true
true blue

this is not my happy face
i'm not in my happy place
because of you
yes because of you
it's all you

it's all about you

it's always all about you

True Fax (at the Stop & Shop°)

Laura's worse for wear
As she passes by the Stop & Shop°
She has no coupons
To redeem at the Stop & Shop°
She's got loads of time
Cause nobody's yet done priced it
So she's just gonna sit
Everyone gets a piece of her mind
She won't love me
Even though she sez she's tried it
She's just gonna drink
Cause she sez I'm too kind

Oh life's so realistic / At the Stop & Shop°
Shrink-wrapped plastic / At the Stop & Shop°
Packages to tantalize / At the Stop & Shop°
Buy Buy Buy Buy / Stop Stop Stop & Shop°

There's True Facts at our disposal
But with pictures of Farrah & Cher
They are what's called People
And they've always got lots to wear
The tunes playing on the A.M
Most are produced by Steve Nicks
I can't seem to understand them
But I guess that's half the trick
Laura's little Paco, who's Seven
Is in love with Donny & Marie
He doesn't understand why the Mormons
Never marry out of the family

Oh life's so realistic / At the Stop & Shop°
Shrinked wrap plastic / At the Stop & Shop°
Packages to tantalize / At the Stop & Shop°
Buy Buy Buy Buy / Stop Stop Stop & Shop°

"Dating yourself, Dave," I can almost hear you say. Yes, yes, ancient history.

The Truth About It All

(Lyrics by David Greenberg & China Moses)

the truth about it all
is elusive abusive
and so damnable a pain
the truth about it all
stare it down kick it down
you got everything to gain
the truth about it all
don't want to can't try to
unnerstand the lies of me
the truth about it all
beats me up tho buttercup
got the game of fight in me

the truth about it all is not all about the truth
there's hurt between the lies and lies between the facts
the who the what the why
why o why

rolling one into another
never lets up never lets go
got to go on and on again
rolling one into another
one mo' pause one mo' breath
it could swish all down the drain
rolling one into another
light my matches torch my fire
need a damn righteous flame
rolling one into another
sad and rude boys toys of boyo boys
such a shame they're all the same

the truth about it all is not all about the truth
there's hurt between the lies and lies between the facts
the who the what the why
why o why

running away from what
all that i want all that i see
just can't seem to believe
running away from what
please please tell me what
what i want and truly need
running away from what
telling only lies trying to hide
from the truth i'ma flying stealth
running away from what
i know it all cos i seen it all
can't try and unnerstand myself

the truth about it all is not all about the truth
there's hurt between the lies and lies between the facts
the who the what the why
why o why

where o where is the why

Another lyrical started as a tweet exchange with the dear Ms. Moses and ended up as a barrage of my verbiage into the imagined mind-field of lost love. Way back when we collaborated on this, China was supposed to be working on a new project, but things like working to pay the rent seem to get in the way. Boy, do I know how that is. Then she lost love, made an album, fell devastated, moved across the channel, divorced, and then her career trajectory aimed upward and onward. I may have the timeline a bit confused, but so you know, she's all good. I told you earlier, she's in Brooklyn now. Anyway, here is the rough draft lyricals for you all to mine for kernels of truth, sadness, disdain, love, and love lost, and for those bits that still get stuck in your craw? Just toothpick 'em out.

Uh Oh Oh No

I've heard the music today
And hits of yesteryear
I don't believe what some say
Although they say it clear—no no no no no oh no

Girls are still the Barbie dolls
Boys are still strong
Barbie though she dresses tough
She still tags along—no no no no no oh no

Now we might change gender
Boys into girls surrender
Girls into boys together
One is still the stronger partner
Uh oh uh oh they'll say—no no no no no oh no

Uh oh oh no
Uh oh oh no
Uh oh no no

I've heard what they say
Today and yesteryear
Underneath they don't believe today
Although they smell the fear—no no no no no oh no

They understand fashion
As a new politic
But really what is fashion
But another trick—to get you into bed
(Background babes: no no no no no oh no)

Girls are still Barbie dolls
Boys are still strong
Barbie though she dresses tough
She still tags along—to get you the head
(Background babes: no no no no no oh no)

Upa War Jazz

All this Upa War Jazz wish it were over
I.D. cards: who was me mother
No more news just videogames
With all our guys knew they took no blame
All this nonsense gotta take cover

There are some whom I want rid
Others I'd like looked into
All of 'em seem to want me dead
Don't know who to start with so

I'll distribute my targets
'Cos my aim is bad
And I might very well forget
And I'm blank when mad

Steal dandy switchblade
For killing I want no more
Then to shave like they do
Down at the Store 24°

All this Upa War Jazz wish it were over
I.D. cards: who was me father
No more news just someone to blame
With all our guys knew they have no shame
All this freakout gotta take cover

This Upa War is no damn good
All this jazz t'do with strangers
Got my cards like I should
No damn good for this hunger

Treat my wounds with new found laws
Ain't helping where it hurts
Nothing no where no more stores
Acid rain to quench my thirst

At night the sky's aflame
So I sit outside with me mate

The Upa's say they take no blame
My girl thinks the color's great

At least it's better'n the waterbed
And mirrors to make love by
We're so far from walking dead
My girl's got sumthin more to try

All this Upa War Jazz wish it were over
I.D. cards: who was me lover
No more news just wanking heads
Orangutans on psycho meds
Making no sense even in voice-over

Vegetable Blues

A.
I got the Vegetable blues
Vegetable vegitable blues (oooze)
Vegetable dues
Vegetable oooze (ooooweeooo)

B.
I'm sitting here like a tomato
I can't sit straight don kno wheh t'go
Must passed out could put onnashow
Nerves not synchronized really dunno

C.
I'm a vegetable oooze
Vegetable blues (oooze)
Vegetable dues
Vegecable blues (glue-oooez)

D.
Vegetable Veccable Color Blue So true t'you Blue blue My ass is blue
Vegetable Vegetab vegetab vegetable Bluuuuuuues (ooweee...[cough...
cough...hack up a loogie]...ooooze)

E.
One time I was coming through the door
Very next moment had vedged onto the floor

F.
My dear ol' vedjie blues Vegetable blues
Like a tomato oooze (ooozelahlahooze)

(Notes: Suggested order AABCBDCEDEF. Sung in a low + muddled
voice though (oooze) and (oooo) and (etc.) and choruses should be in
a Robert Plant/LedZep falsetto. To have your coughs and hacking be
authentic as possible, drink a pint of Jack Daniels and smoke a whole
pack of Camels before attempting a performance of the song; perhaps
start during the writing of the music to get into the full self-destructive
mood.)

Venus De Mellow

She was a disaster she was a fright
She was the very definition of a never ending night
If only she could be a Venus de mellow

She didn't look back she tore apart my heart
She was pedal to the metal from the very start
If only she could be a Venus de mellow

I fell for her she believed in me
Saw me for what I was
Not what others see in me
So in love for a moment or two
A fantastic kind of love
Then she became unglued
If only she could be a Venus de mellow

She burned so bright she was so hot
Made new friends for hitting this jackpot
If only she could be a Venus de mellow

She was desire our hearts on fire
I had no intuition she was my funeral pyre
If only she could be a Venus de mellow

She didn't look back she tore apart my heart
She was pedal to the metal from the very start
If only she could be a Venus de mellow

I was pondering life after listening to Stacey Kent's song, "La Venus du mélo." I had first thought that her Venus was of the artist, Milo, but in my usual outside-the-box way of thinking, I was popping thoughts around in my brain about being Milo, then mellow, and then not being mellow. Then I Google-translated—the song is in French—and Stacey had been playing with Milo/Mélo, as in a "Venus of melodrama." But I was already off in a world of my own, remembering this walking disaster of a girl—you must know at least one—and how the world might be a better, calmer, place if she were less of a never-ending nightmare, though mellow, while good for Donovan, would not have been so inspirational.

Walking Hat

If the shoe fits, wear it
If the hat fits, take it
But as Max Ernst said, watch it
For a hat can walk away

Do a little walking hat on a sunny day
Walk away hat
Walk away

Wasting Time At Maureen's

All I heard them say
All I heard them say
All I heard them say
Was grow up boy
We're just looking for a thinking man

Come to think of it I couldn't think
They had plugged my brains into the sink
And tied my hands with yesterday's Times
Though stuffed my mouth with sweets (so kind)

All I heard them say
All I heard them say
All I heard them say
Was grow up boy
We're just looking for a few good men

Then they played with Maureen as if a toy
Up or down like she had a choice
They had on my Father's old suit and socks
While stealing the hands off Grandfather's clocks

Now they tell me go punch the clocks
Punch the clocks
Punch the clocks
Punch the clocks

Clocks got no hands and I've none in stock
None in stock
None in stock
None in stock

Look no hands Ma, but all the time in the world

All I heard them say
All I heard them say
All I heard them say

Was grow up boy
We're just looking for a self-made man

They took all my money to feed the poor
Got none now to get anything more
Newsies tell me freedom's just hype
Just another word they have set in cold type

All I heard them say
All I heard them say
All I heard them say
Was punch the clocks
We're just looking for a real good time

Radio was left to tell me the future
Human interest stuff like what's cute or
The Top of the Pops and Action News at Six
Can't really tell if it's really news at six

Clocks got no hands and I've none in stock
None in stock
None in stock
None in stock

Now I'm told to go punch the clocks
Punch the clocks
Punch the clocks
Punch the clocks

Wet Smiles Of A Summer Night

Under rain the night sounds cool
As Sara's whispers fall
As midsummer rain slides cool
Against sweaty walls

The street slickens inviting
Fog to slip across
Sara smiles a smile inviting
Another summer kiss

Wet smiles of a summer night wet smiles
Wet smiles of words so light wet smiles
A little night music
As fog slips across the rain slickened street
Caressing time

The night smiles slowly upon us
With rain like fresh dew
Raindrops meeting at the kiss
And the night sounds so new

(Night sounds improvisational jam)

Wet smiles of a summer night wet smiles
Wet smiles of words so light wet smiles
A little night music
As fog slips across the rain slickened street
Caressing time

We've Got The Power

(Lyrics by David Greenberg and Del Bartle / Music by Del Bartle)

Don't need your pity or your petty prayers
That crap won't heal us, doesn't show you care
Self-serving and deceitful without a shadow of doubt
We've got the power
To kick you gangsters out

Silver spooned to excess never worked a day
Toadies at your side you tweet the world away
Daddy's money, hooker honeys; laughing at us, ain't it funny
We've got the power ......
To vote you chancers out

Well you can talk of liberty and freedom as if it's under duress
Read our mail behind the veil, neglect our choices, always putting
loyalty to the test
The game is to neglect our protests, yes we're snowflakes at best
Try to criminalize our bedrooms, take control of our sex
We've got the power ......
To cut you bankers out

Pontificating, misinforming hacks
Sugar coated lies dressed up; alternative facts
Defenders of the realm, we can do without
We've got the power ....
To vote you fuckers out

You can find the video of this on YouTube. The "band" is almost all Del except
for our vocalist who shall remain nameless because of all the right-winged trolls
who terrorize her online for speaking her mind. So far, it's the only video in the
Vote Them Out account. It's not like Del and I haven't been pissed off about
anything since, just these things take a goddamn bit of time that we don't have
enough of to spend. We tried to have this go viral in 2020, but it does come in
handy every election season since, as it seems there's almost a never-ending
parade of Fascists who want to jackboot democracy into submission.

What Do Boys Want?

(Chorus:)
What do boys want what do girls want
You can ask them you can tell them
All they say is I dunno, I know
What do boys want what do girls want
You can ask them you can tell them
All they say is I dunno, I know

Danny wants the price of a nice device
To help him out
Danny wants the price of a nice device
To help him out
He stays all day
His bills he won't pay
He won't go away
Go away boy go away

Go to hell and play—go away

(Chorus)

Sammy wants a girl who'll twirl his curls
Behind his ears
Sammy wants a girl who'll twirl his curls
Behind his ears
He looks in bars
He looks in cars
He'll journey long and far
For sex he'll starve

Starving for some action—starving

(Chorus)

Robbie wants a lover who's undercover
Not like her husband
Robbie wants a lover who's undercover

Not like her husband
She writes to magazines
Brushes with Gleem
Her smile just steams
Any machismo schemes

Steaming the shirts straight—damn straight

(Chorus)

Maggy wants the life of another wife
Who don't cook so much
Maggy wants the life of another wife
Who don't clean too much
She feels such a slave
And not one bit brave
To head into the waves
And kiss it all away

Kiss her life a dark goodbye—kiss it lightly

What do boys want what do girls want
You can ask them you can tell them
And all they say is I dunno—they know
And all they say is I dunno—they know

They damn well know—just not saying so

What I Want

i want to tell you thoughts unkind
i want to tell you i've lost my mind
i want to tell you how much i hurt
i want to tell you give me back my shirts

breaking what i thought i lost
breaking what i thought i gained
breaking all the ties that bind
just breaking down

i want to kiss you but i refrain
i want to kiss you i'm blind with pain
i want to kiss you but there's no fire
i want to kiss you but lost all desire

the cup from your mom, the last eggs we bought together, the binder
clips, on the road and fear and loathing, pens, pencils, paper clips, pads
and envelopes, the arts fest prize from who knows who, the coffee tin,
the bills you paid, the bills just came in, the toaster that worked okay,
sea shells that you adored, birthday cards, some gingermints found on
the floor, your phone, your scarves, your toiletries, the days and nights
we were best, the fights, the words you threw like daggers, the scrap-
books that held it all together, can't get them back, can't get them back,
can't get them back, jeez

the lamp we bought in paris
is in leeetle pieces on the floor
your precious donald duck figurine
sadly is no more

ripped up your magazines
tore apart your letters
i'm so freaking tired
but i feel so much better

breaking what i thought i lost
breaking what i thought i gained

breaking all the ties that bind
just breaking down

i want to tell you back stabber
i want to tell you money grabber
i want to tell you you're so absurd
i want to tell you but i'll mangle the words

breaking what i thought i lost
breaking what i thought i gained
breaking all the ties that bind
just breaking down

Sent this lyrical off years ago to the studios of Del Bartle's Credible Hulk
Productions when he was based over in the UK. I met Del when he worked at
Rykodisc's London office. At present, he is guitarist/writer at The Citizens Of
Nowhere & The Converters and formerly of The Sid Presley Experience, The
Godfathers, and The Unholy Trinity. Del emailed back: *it's going in a sort of mid-
pace deranged electro-rock vibe!* I asked, *But can you dance to it?*

Still waiting for a reply and a glimmer of something in return. I forgot about
sending this off to him until I wedged it into this updated edition. Since I'm still
waiting, these many many years later, and he's since moved himself, wife and
guitars, to California, maybe I'll send him an email or two or three. Or maybe
a signed copy of the folio to wink, wink, nudge him along. If you glance back
at "We've Got The Power," you'll see that Del and I did get at least one of our
collabs finished and recorded under our nom de guerre, Mothers of Exile.

What You Want

Call me what you want
If I wear my heart on my sleeve
And If I believe love is love
Not a daisy chain of infidelities

Give me your heart
Not a passing glance
And you'll have more than
Half a chance

Give me what you will
Some half-baked lies
Got to be kidding
Don't even try

Give me some attention
Uh-huh doesn't cut it
Want more of this show me
Some spirit

Call me what you want
If I want so much more than this hell
If I believe love his love
Not an afternoon of kiss and tell

Give me no more stories
Give me no more lies
All your little fictions
End with goodbye

What you want is what I need
A little bit of love and a lot of belief
What you want is what I crave
Someone to love me someone to behave

Give me the love I need
Not your fancy diamonds and pearls

Guilty pleasures after running
With some girls

Call me what you want
If I wear my heart on my sleeve
And If I believe love is love
Not a daisy chain of infidelities

Give me your heart
Not a passing glance
And you'll have more than
Half a chance

Why Are You Staring At Me?

I don't know what's going on
I just know it's wrong
Someone is lying
Someone is spying on me

Why are you staring at me
Don't use your eyes that way
Why are you staring like that at me
What have you got to say

Your eyes a Revlon® factory
Your face is a mystery
You sit and wonder
Why your life is a blunder

You just sit staring at me

I don't know what's going on
I just know that it's wrong
Someone is lying
Someone is spying on me

Why are you staring at me
I don't know just that I see
Someone wholly different
Someone different than me

Why are you staring at me
I don't know what it is you see
Someone is lying
Someone is spying on me

Why You Can't Load The Dishwasher Dear

like sand in the gears of a spinning machine
not helping, you're not helping
mud on the floor of a floor I just cleaned
not helping, you're not helping
racheting me down as I get higher
not helping, you're not helping
I'm so frustrated I always seem tired
not helping, you're not helping

water and a hydroplaning car in distress
not helping, you're not helping
my derriere in a cocktail party dress
not helping, you're not helping
when my triple soy latte tastes of curdled milk
not helping, you're not helping
that look my mother gives and my jewish guilt
not helping, you're not helping

you scrape it you stack it there's a way to rack it
admit it admit it just don't throw a fit
your way of tossing them leaves me very wary
architected goo like that guy gehry
they'll still be dirty they won't be clean
it's so wrong it's almost mean
it's enough to leave me depressed
like when my derriere
is in that
cocktail
party
dress

state troopers and their radar guns when i'm running late
not helping, you're not helping
that little burp and you're friends can guess what you ate
not helping, you're not helping
a crack in the windshield and nails in the tire
not helping, you're not helping

do not want this job anymore how can i get fired
not helping, you're not helping

water and a hydroplaning car in distress
not helping, you're not helping
my derriere in a cocktail party dress
not helping, you're not helping
when my triple soy latte tastes of curdled milk
not helping, you're not helping
that look my mother gives and my jewish guilt
not helping, you're not helping

Wind (the sound of crying)

Knifing through the still air of night
The phoenix has a powerful flight
Over the moonlit valleys and screams—silent

They fly strong yet nameless
Leaving winds where windless
Alighting on the forks of trees—silent

Before they're about to expire
They build their own funeral pyre
And from this oven they alight—triumphant

The phoenix begins again their flight
Searching for a name without sight
Or a clue to where they've flown—so silent

I know who I am at least I have a name
Yet I can't be so sure I'll be back
After I die
When I ask you to lie beside me here
I can't remember where I've been
Or where I lie
You hide my fears eat my thoughts steal my name
But I know how to coax them back
And make you fly

Flying over the silent dreams
Of winding windless streams
Flying till you cry out—silent

Falling back silently back
The moon is sailing at what we lack
Like the phoenix we burn again—silent

We leave melodies there wordless
Together as one nameless
We weave a tapestry of flight—so silent

I know who I am at least I have a name

Yet I can't be so sure I'll be back
After I die
When I ask you to lie beside me here
I can't remember where I've been
Or where I lie
You hide my fears eat my thoughts steal my name
But I know how to coax them back
And make you fly

And cry silent
To reach out for the phoenix
The sound silent
A fugue upon the wind to forget
But know how to knife—the wind

Words For Everything

got some words for our love together
it was so cool and so was the weather
got some words for the summer we spent
3 short months ever gonna pay the rent
got some words for the sand in our shorts
mmmmm baby (pause) it was worth it

got some words for the breakfasts you made
looked like cardboard and tasted like raid
got some words for your mom and your dad
dropping in and calling first isn't so bad
got some words for them finding us like that
mmmmm baby (pause) it was worth it

got some words for the time of my life
been a long strange trip you got that right
got some words for this half-assed song
read between the lines tho it won't be long
got some words for the girls you slept with
mmmmm baby (pause) was it worth it

got words for everything
got words for everything
but got nothing in the book and i looked and looked
got no words about
got no words about
what to do next

got some words for our love together

(audience participation time: ask them what words they'd use to de-
scribe a guy who kinda good, but went so bad... etc. play with them back
and forth...if it's not that kinda crowd, then:)
(humm like you're thinking of sumthin to sing)
mmmmmmmmmmmmmmmm....stormy weather
got some words for the summer we spent
(if they are really into it, let the audience rip into "him" here or)

drove my ride thanks for bleeping dent
got some words for the sand in our shorts
mmmmm baby (pause) it was worth it

got words for everything
got words for everything
they even got a word for one who fakes a smile
and one for passion most pathological
and even one for (break/spoken:) the use of foul or abusive language to
relieve stress or easing pain
(back to singing:) but got nothing in the book and i looked and looked
got no words about
got no words about
what to do next

+ + + + + + + + +

(And in case anyone asks...
Faking a smile: eccedentesiast
Swearing to ease pain: lalocheziaa
Continued passion/unyielding disease: aeipathy—ah so love is a sick-
ness as well as a drug. Excellent.)

I cribbed the idea for this lyrical from an EP by Merrily James titled, yup, *Words
For Everything*. Please head on over to wherever you consume your music right
now to check out her tracks. Merrily James. Yes, Merrily. Though don't stay out
there too long. Please come back to finish the rest of the folio. Maybe one day,
Ms. James will be inspired to write music for the words her EP title inspired. As
this lyric is now nearly a teenager, the words are most definitely not where her
head is these days. So maybe not. Merrily finished her EP when she was one of
my interns at that company which still shall not be named. This was so last job
ago; I have moved on in the past decade, and she as well, composing more fine
music and exquisitely found her own words for a lot of everything else. Look her
up, Merrily. James.

Wrong Kind Of Sorry

skin on skin not letting you in
delighted you've been slighted
you're the wrong kind of sorry

your head fakes sorry for god's sake
demanding truth in a g-string
you're the wrong kind of sorry

lip service a new shade of bliss
gossipy flirt you own the real hurt
you're the wrong kind of sorry

she lives well everything's swell
dreams seem a translucent hell
you're the wrong kind of sorry

sorry sorry sorry sorry are we
you're the wrong kind of sorry
fallen angels thirst for gossip in the gutter of sorry street
clip your wings oh you'll be sorry

you're the wrong kind
you're the wrong kind
you're the wrong kind
you're the wrong kind
you're the wrong kind
you're the wrong kind

lines in sand deny all demands
trampling trust sympathy and lust
you're the wrong kind of sorry

poison lips switchblade finger tips
love is vain when you jack your claim
you're the wrong kind of sorry

french blissing constantly dissing

all the ways you bang yesterdays
you're the wrong kind of sorry

skin on skin not letting you in
delighted you've been slighted
you're the wrong kind of sorry

sorry sorry sorry sorry are we
you're the wrong kind of sorry
sorry sorry sorry sorry
sorry

Not a state of affairs from the recent past, so don't you worry. Be happy. Yet use
your outdoor voice.

Yet We Dare

garbage on the highway
who knows what crap's in the air
fucking with mother nature
we should be really really scared

truth or dare
we should care
yet we dare

give us yr poor and downtrodden
teach them how to play unfair
crushing their devotion
we should be really really scared

truth or dare
we should care
yet we dare

stealing votes stuffing ballots
[break/spoken: these are not the votes you are looking for]
we the people aren't spared
stand dumbndumber and callous
we should be really really scared

truth or dare
we should care
yet we dare

disrobing sweet justice
have2have our fair share
tipping her scales with malice
we should be really really scared

truth or dare
we should care
yet we dare

(break/boprap:)
dare2scheme our pretty petty dreams want want want but can't can't
can't our ways with means means our ways are mean our dervish whirl
makes a selfish world unhappiness reigns down on me and you a hard
reign's gonna fall for us all dare-ling you know what's true for me and for
you you you you and me me me self-less would be better but it's easier
2dare2scheme our pitiful petty dreams

and so daring so we dare

tagging names with a number
erasing faces in despair
gag orders steal their thunder
we should be really really scared

truth or dare
we should care
yet we dare

keep them kick them down
faceless / sexless w/out a prayer
dimming their sense of wonder
we should be really really scared

truth or dare
we should care
yet we dare

Man, how I wish I were more connected in the biz of music as this lyrical was as
topical as the news blaring out of NPR every hour on the hour the day I started
this one—inspiring me to set down the first few lines and then some more later,
and then after pondering it through errands, and overnight, it was done. This
song is ready for target practice, sung and heard in the *Here & Now*—yes, also
the name of a local Boston NPR show—and not hanging around here in the
comfort of this book. So stop lollygagging; you lyricals you.

You Promised

Love you promised
Sunny skies you promised
You promised to take me to that promised land
Love you guaranteed
Better than could ever be
You promised much that was out of your hands

You promised love
Health and happiness weren't far behind
I believed
Hanging on to all I heard
Exodus
In leaving you weren't very kind
You promised love
Until you grabbed back your very word

Life you promised
A family you promised
A promise to build upon that promised land
Marriage guaranteed
Better than could ever be
You promised much that was out of your hands

There's no guarantee that can guarantee a guarantee
But I need a guarantee that when you leave you'll leave
For good
For good
For good

Love you promised
Sunny skies you promised
You promised to take me to that promised land
Love you guaranteed
Better than could ever be
Your promises always slipping out of your hands

You'll Remember Me

When tomorrow is yesterday
Blowing past another birthday
Everyone singing way off-key
You'll remember me

When your teachers call your name
Looking to find the one to blame
When you try to hide your glee
You'll remember me

Hoping on cars driving on by
Counting the airplanes in the sky
When there's no possibility
You'll remember me

You'll remember me like I need to
Though I hope you'll treat them better than I did you
I promise I'll be back someday soon
A trouble of knots that I can't undo
Someone will get hurt if I stay
I know that's true

Please remember me
Like I will you
Please remember me
Like I will you
I will love you always
Yes I will
That's one promise I can't undo

When you finally kiss the bride
And find you're on the wrong ride
Blinded by her love indeed
You'll remember me

Head over heels you'll fall for her
Made in heaven as it were

When you can't give her all she needs
You'll remember me

Love her as you promised
Tell her no lies try to be honest
When you screw up and plead
You'll remember me

(Bridge)
Nothing lasts forever there's always an end of the line
Will you be whatever regretting how you did your time
A bitter surrender to toe the middle and just be fine
When you can deliver the extraordinary and really shine

You'll remember me like I need to
Though I hope you'll treat them better than I did you
I promise I'll be back someday soon
A trouble of knots that I can't undo
Someone will get hurt if I stay
I know that's true

Love her as you promised
Tell her no lies try to be honest
When you screw up and plead
That's when you'll remember me

You're Not Jesus Or Jesus Saves (Plaid Stamps®)

Liar—you're not my messiah
I don't understand your head
Please—don't try to preach to me
I'm tired and I want to go to bed
Lord—frankly, I'm getting bored
With your psalms of grateful dead

Please—I don't need another religion
And I don't think you're Jesus Christ
I can use—my own head to make decisions
And my own money to pay the price

What you don't seem to understand
Is that I for one don't need a new religion
That your frantic sleight of hand
Will never win the wars that need to be won

Liar—you're not my messiah
I don't need to understand your head
Please—don't try to preach to me
I'm tired and I want to go to bed
Lord—frankly I'm getting bored
With your psalms of grateful dead

Liar—you're not my messiah
And I don't think you're Jesus Christ

You're One

you're one to say i don't care
when you're the one who's never there
you're one to say let's not fight
when you're the one who's not home at night
you're one and it takes two

you're one to say we fell out of love
when you're the one who's kissing someone new
you're one to say i'm the liar
when you're the one who's never ever been true
you're one and it takes two

you're one to say it's over
when you're the one who made me love you from the start
you're one to feel there's no romance
when you're the one who's torn apart my heart
you're one and it takes two

you're one to say i'm dishonest
when you're the one who's wrapped up in lies
you're one to say i'm not in love
when you're the one with hate in your eyes
you're one and it takes two

you're one to say i'm heartless
you're one to say i'm vicious
you're one to say i'm bitter
you're one to say i'm the reason
i'm not wrong and i'm not right
i'm the one who's getting even

you're one to say i've failed you
when you add one plus one and equal three
you're one to say i'm bitter
when you've chopped down the family tree
you're one and it takes two

takes two to mess it up takes two to fight the fight
it takes two to be so wrong for each other
if you're wrong for me then i'm so wrong for you
it takes one to know one and only one of us is right

you're one to say we threw it all away
when you're the one who's been sleeping around
you're one to say i'm a house wrecker

when you're the one with lipstick traces on your frown
you're one and it takes two

takes two to mess it up takes two to fight the fight
takes two to be so wrong for each other
if you're wrong for me then i'm so wrong for you
and how can two wrongs ever make it right

you're one to say i'm heartless
you're one to say i'm vicious
you're one to say i'm bitter
you're one to say i'm the reason
i'm not wrong and i'm not right
i'm the one who's getting even

you're one and it takes two

takes two to mess it up takes two to fight the fight
takes two to be so wrong for each other
if you're wrong for me then i'm so wrong for you
and how can two wrongs ever make it right

Zero-Zero-One-One-Two

It's a deaf trip and I can't keep my eyes off of you
Your stockings show off your two-=inch high heeled shoes
It makes you taller so you can see on the other side
It's a mute trip and I really can't believe my eyes

It's been too long since I last lost my sense of wonder
Everyone I know has changed into someone other

It's a deaf trip
It's a mute trip
And there's too much to see
It's a mute trip
It's a deaf trip
And much too little to believe

It's a blind way with nothing to really see
Stockholding images playing fancy with the mind
Planting platforms on the bottoms of your feet
Once were medicine now are the fashion sign

It's a deaf trip
It's a mute trip
And there's too much to see
It's a mute trip
It's a deaf trip
And much too little to believe

A short breath
I really can't breathe but I should take one more
A lame trip
I'm two inches taller but my feet are sore
Erased tape
My ears are blind and I can't see my eyes
A short breath
I'm still waiting for the whisper of the skies

The Machine Gun Rag

Ahh, yes, this little piece was stirred up by the Youth Rebellion of the Yippies, the Weathermen, the S.D.S., the Black Panthers who held court in the 1960s. I was enthralled with them, even though just a teen. You have seen the movies and read the books; I don't need to write down all the shit they were fighting against, as it was a multi-layered platform created by disparate groups and best read in books by pundits or historians.

The Man, and his wingman J. Edgar Hoover, tried to tamp all this down. However, the 1970s still saw unrest as the young radicals tried to tear apart the crappy status quo Nixon and others were holding steadfast to maintain. This so-called revolution was not the Hollywood nihilism of bad boy Brando in *The Wild One* scripted to shock the old fogies.

What are you rebelling against, Johnny?

Whaddaya got?

Those wild ones became parents and the next generation had definitive targets, defined issues. The Left aimed their protest and, yes, used violence to right the wrongs, to bring justice to its rightful place: for all. Anger was simmering, then exploded at Kent State, Jackson State, Camden, NJ. The through-line was clear; the oppressed against the oppressors. Good versus bad. Us against The Man.

As FZ sang, *Brown shoes don't make it.*

Though, when the Symbionese Liberation Army came to the forefront of the news in '74—especially when Ms. Patty Hearst took on her Tania role—when the S.L.A. started shooting up banks and such, it seemed to me that the Left took a wrong turn at Sense and Sensibility Streets. Or, at least, these Leftists. What the hell were they thinking? In those hip and happening 1970s, all the fuckwad assholes at my high school were dressing up hippy and hipster or funkadelic. Looking way cool, but still dickweeds through and through, clothes as costumes, or as Zappa told one heckler, *Everybody in this room is wearing a uniform, don't kid yourself.*

The S.L.A. were anarchists parading as revolutionaries, in love with their own enthusiasm for creating unrest and chaos, in love with the sound of firing machine guns, not so much to change the status quo, but rather for the thrill of holding up banks so they could grab the money and run.

I was sketching out a film script I called *Coney Island* around then. The premise of that flick had the insurgents tooling around Manhattan in clown suits, blowing up banks and other governmental buildings. Scribbling about a revolution: I was all for change but on the fence; you could count me not out and yet not in, like Lennon, but you could color me freaking perplexed at why anyone fighting for a new society would take guns to innocents. That was the modus operandi of the Government, the Army, and the National Guard. The Man.

Then again, what if the rhetoric spouted was flowing from a beautiful girl? One with a sensual voice, long hair, psychedelic leggings under a micro-mini skirt, lips looking especially sweet, one with whom you thought there might be a chance, as she was focusing all her beatific energy on pulling you, the wary, onto her side? Under those taxing conditions, my high-school self might have listened to an evening or two of Mao, hopefully, in my fevered mind, next to her, under her sheets.

And so therein lies the basis for these three songs forming the scant outline of the concept album I envisioned rising from the ashes of Patty Hearst's escapades.

By the way, in the sub-basement under the mini-pantheon of Tape Dave Music history, you'll find the filecard noting it was one of these three long diatribes making up "The Machine Gun Rag" which unnerved the guys in the jazz-rock instrumental band. A chain reaction of moments ensued, causing "Walking Hat," that briefest reverie of a lyrical, to be scribbled then and there.

Again, the band had no vocalist being all instrumental. So any size of lyrical abandon would be way too much for them, which was also the case with "Walking Hat."

Machine Gun Rag 1: Informal Interview

She invited me up into her dreams
Asked me what they all mean
I told her I was no Joseph

I wore no manly colored cloak
Just a work shirt and jeans

She invited me up into her room
Asked me to mop up with a broom
I told her I was no workingman
Even though I wore the clothes
I'd get out as fast as I can

She asked me questions
Like I was a prophet or a sage
But all I read was "Masterplots"
And really had not turned a page

She asked me questions
That were too much to bear
I had no notes to fall back on
No character really there

She wanted to join "the revolution"
I told her "no revolution here"
She wanted to join right away
I asked her to please go away

I asked her if her Dad knew
Who and where she was
She said don't say a word
Or they would contact the "fuzz"

The place would soon be crawling
With Locusts from the plague
That would descend from heaven
But she was rather vague

Who were these Locusts
The cops or maybe Narcs
Or maybe even Moby Dick
Or the mysterious white shark

Keep your questions under your hat
In your pocket

Keep your money in the bank
Save your locket

Save your years – go back home
Wait to grow up
Tell dad you love him – kiss his nose
Wait to mature

She asked me questions
Like I was a prophet or a sage
She was incoherent
She was rather vague

She handed me her picture
The one with Mom and Dad
Then the one with her machine gun
Her alibi was iron clad
She looked very muscular
An athlete from the Olympiad
Poised and sprouting revolution
Direct from Stalingrad

She invited me up to dream
Of a future that ended in farce
She punctuated with bullets
And with breaths that were sparse

Keep your money
Keep your money
Keep your hard earned pay
We don't need it
We don't need it
Why don't you go away

Keep your beliefs
Keep your future
Keep it locked away
Keep your Mommy
Keep your Daddy
Why don't you go away

She insisted that she stay
She could pay her own way

She invited me up—into her dreams
And asked me what they mean
She invited me up—to dust and mop
And war her set of jeans

She asked me her scripted questions
That she bought from the Post

She rifled me of my podium
And served wine and the host

She thought I was the future
I could change rearrange
With me as her pointer
Maybe she could
She thought she would

She asked me questions
She asked me questions
Like I was a prophet or a sage
She asked me questions
Of my shoe size and nocturnal age

She was incoherent babbling of the plague
That would soon come she was rather vague

She asked me questions
That were too much to bear
I had no notes to fall back on
No character really there

She wanted to join the revolution
I told her "No revolution here"
She was incoherent babbling of the plague
She wore a mask was it here she was rather vague

She wanted to join right away today
I asked her to please / Please go / Please go away

Machine Gun Rag II: The Siamese Libidinous Navy (Or Anchor's Aweigh Tania)

A restless hemi bicarb of the elm tree set
Using her live bait as her pet
Always letting her pet sit on her lap

Beneath the golden halo on her head
She smiles like a hunter who shoots the dead
Instinctively she lays her traps

She tries to understand the universe
From the tightness of her purse
From the pursed lips that are chapped

Broken nails from her feet dot the floor
Dirty baby hands dot the whiteness of the door
And she sits in the middle of the crap

Sitting, rarely living
Giving only when she can
Living, rarely staying
Awake only if she can

She laughed like a stop sign spectator
Then raised up her machine gun
And started laughing when she shot like it was fun

But it seems
She doesn't know what living is
She walks talks
But she doesn't know what's going down
Sitting, barely living
Going only when she can
Living, rarely staying
Awake if she only can

She preaches yet rarely listens
Her ears are stuffed with prophets

She doesn't know what she's missing
But she scores well on F.B.I targets

She's aimed at you
But she doesn't know what you stand for
She's aimed at you
She can't distinguish her platform from her floor

She's aimed at you
Right on target between the eyes
She's aimed at you
And she'll pretend to really die

Sitting, rarely living
Going only when she can
Living, rarely staying
Awake if she only can

But it seems
She doesn't know what living is
She walks talks
But she doesn't know what's going down

Beneath the golden halo on her head
She smiles like a hunter who shoots the dead
Instinctively she lays her traps

She laughed like a stop sign spectator
Then raised up her machine gun
And started laughing when she shot like it was fun

Machine Gun Rag III: Peppermint Patty & The Tapes

Snakes coiled in tight fitting blue jeans
Awaiting the chance to tell
Their mouths awake at the seams
Awaiting the chance to yell

The microphone is plugged in

And Patty reads her speech
Her fingers caress the windscreen
Tries to underground preach

When I was a young kid
I used to listen to everything anybody said
I believed it all too
I'm much older now
And I don't want to listen (you hear what I said)
I mean it all too

Your thoughts are not mine
So why should I listen to your opinion
Please tell me why
But I want you to listen
I want you to sit down and listen
I don't have to tell you why

For the first time
Patty really feels alive even though drugged
She believed it all too
But seeing is believing
And it's on the action plan (doing it all)
Doing 'til it's do or die

Now she doesn't want to listen
She wants to spout her own opinion
And what if you don't want to hear
You just turn your head and you're dead

Because if you own a factory
Or even a clothing store
They've got bombs they've got money
They've got ideas they'll blow you up for sure

Because you don't want to listen
Just because they don't like your face

As to the order of things

Instead of lazily stacking the writings in order, all in a neat timeline, chronologi-
cally marching to the finish: youngster to oldster, naïve poseur to Samuel Beckett
wannabe, unpublished dude to, well, still unpublished dude—forget the last one,
and I guess the Beckett one before that is not much of a difference either. So, yes,
instead of just going on automatic, I wanted to have the lyrics present themselves
to you, dear reader, in a new fantastic assemblage. Perhaps to hide any sort of
progression, growth, or conversely, to show off, perhaps...the declining side of the
bell curve degenerating into infantilism, or pointing out something worse; that of,
gahd, could it be, maybe, oh dear, artistic stagnation?

Perhaps.

Actually, I hate the logic of the chronologically inclined. Or the non-
thought that goes behind it. Musical compilations that tie the individual tracks'
ordering to the release date give no sense of the artistic stream of consciousness
that created the recordings. And chronological to what is a good question. The
songs may have been written ages before and remixed and released ages later—
the same with poetry compilations listing the poems in dated order. When the
writings were published may have nothing to do with when they were written or
when they were written has nothing to do with when they were first thought, or
the inspirations lying hidden underneath the subtext which could, perhaps, string
them into a new daisy chain.

I wanted a new order as I find great power in juxtapositions, strange
segues, abrupt stops, or even slow dissolves through themes. While producing
CD compilations for Rykodisc, I worked hard to figure out a journey the tracks
and the listener would finally take on the release. Some sequences were almost
seamless, just barely felt changes, escalator-smooth excursions to the next mood.
Others were like sharp drops from tropical rainforests into icy mountain lakes. It all
depended on the overall soundscape I was ultimately trying to create, the journey
I wanted the listeners to take.

Before that life, while working in the film biz, it was a revelation to try
different scenes and sounds against one another to refine or change or destroy

or pray it would fix the film. A mistake that worked, an experiment so totally out of the box that fit so right, was unexpected. It was a jab at my then sense of "professional." That I always knew how to do the right thing, what I learned in film school and how I got my union card. Perhaps there is some skill in taking the experiments and making them work, understanding how they work. Still, some degree of chance made the whole game more exciting.

In the 1970s, Brian Eno and Peter Schmidt codified their own accidental methods of creativity with a series of cards called *Obique Strategies; one hundred worthwhile dilemmas*. Eno would use the deck to help point out his next move, when stuck within a project. With cards like "Be dirty "or "Remove specifics and convert to ambiguities" pulled out of the deck, Eno and his compatriots would ponder the words as both the creative idea as well as the strategy to help them push on through to the next artistic step. (I had these suckers as an app on the web, but it was weirdly gone when I compiled the first folio. A new version is now on the iPhone App Store and Eno's site has an expanded edition of the cards.)

With the *Mud Folio*, I wanted to insert new juxtapositions and themes with a different running order, but I really didn't want to revisit the works with that amount of detail to think it through. I wanted to see new cooler than thou juxtapositions happen and have the readers (hopefully more than a handful) take new routes through the work. But it was mind-numbing to even get to the point to figure out where to start, and then the looming sheer amount of work that lay ahead stalled me ever so; the idea of ever seeing the first edition of thing published vanished.

Use the cards, I thought. However, even with those in hand, it still felt excruciating. I dreaded going back to sift through the stack of papers to reconfigure new moods and themes. Especially after all the lyrics from my intimately scrawled and ultimately sprawling notebooks took so long to be word-processed—and even with that, I had help thanks to Sarah and Michael. No way. And it seemed too precious (and expensive) to have an editor sift through them all and create a new order out of the massive stack of stuff.

Yes, I could have thrown them down the proverbial and literal staircase. But that involved the actuality of picking the pages up and restacking and reshuffling. Still way too much work. Or I could have given them to kindergartners to throw around, play with, and hand them back to me after class, all sticky and crinkly but pleasantly jumbled. Although god forbid if and when their parents, or teachers, saw some of the words from the lyrics...not that they're "gangsta" or anything, they're just not for "youngstas!" I was in the funk of a whole different level of writer's block, an impasse I couldn't hurdle over and move on with my lyrical life. Then I remembered Elvis Costello coming out with a songbook entitled *Elvis Costello, A Singing Dictionary*.

It was in alphabetical order.

There it was, my solution; chance connections via the sort function of MS Word with not one bit of heavy lifting or additional thinking on my part. The order was free of my intervention, my preconceived notions of what the lyrics meant, and how they would fit with, or crash into, the next one. Which was what I wanted have to happen but didn't want to create; a new order of possibilities untouched by this human's hands. That's why a song with an ellipsis starts this whole shenanigans and why the lyrics all are stitched together the way they are; the somewhat random act of titling led to the final order of this book.

I did decide to rip one set of lyrics out of this automated process and insert them as the end piece. Not because they were the best, or the funniest, or anything other than they are themost extensive lyrics I have written to date.

"The Machine Gun Rag" is a series of three lyricals—the hint of an operetta that I fashioned after a spate of concept albums fell into my life, like *Aqualung*, or *We're Only In It For The Money*. My thought on removing this weighty and massive verbiage to the end was this: if "The Machine Gun Rag" came in the middle of the book, it would drag the whole enterprise of reading to a dead stop. That is, if anyone was taking the time to read these lyricals one by one, instead of cherry-picking the titles, or maybe tossing the book down their own staircases to see on which page the book landed.

The heft and weight of those songs made me relegate my teenage take of the Patty Hearst and the Symbionese Liberation Army saga to the butt-end of the *Mud Folio* after the alphabetical order had duly run its course. Mostly it was to spare the reader from making his/her/their own choice of whether to wade in during the initial read-through or check it out at the end.

A very suitable placement since I feel humorless anarchists should be at the butt-end of jokes, though they are rarely put there. Perhaps due to the armaments they carry, or they won't get the joke and be offended. Or both. If I were a betting man, I would put my money down on their use of (guns, bombs, knives, insert your evil and ultra-violent weapon of choice here) to attack the erstwhile jokester, since being both humorless and revolutionaries, they can never get the joke. But that's a sucker's bet.

Of course, they would use violence. And sacrificial lambs. They know no other language than that of violence to put themselves ahead. Because they are right and everyone else is wrong, they would kill almost everyone else in the world. Not an excellent method to gain converts to their cause or build an audience for their teachings, but definitively an efficient way to kill a joke. Imagine, with no one else left in the world, they would have to clean up their own messes as well as ours. So, perhaps, the joke is on them?

If the revolutionaries were genuinely trying to create a new and better future for the world, it would be a very surreal future. They are doing no better than the polluters whose technologically advanced gadgets make the world a more comfortable place to live within while cramming crap into the sky and rivers, creating a stinkier, smog-filled, acid-rained upon earth—a deadlier place in which to use those devices engineered to fulfill the promise of a better life.

Revolutionaries, it is the back of the book with you. And if you have a problem with that, let me ask one tiny question: why are you reading a book of silly little lyricals anyway? And if you have read all the ways to this end page and didn't even crack a smile? Then to hell with you because guess what? That's the cosmic joke of it all. We're all going to the heaven or hell of our choosing, and if you think you're going to a quiet, peaceful place after all your violent acts of anger and aggression, no matter how well you justify them in your head-crafted worldview, think again.

Think hard. And think again. In fact, Bad Guys, while thinking, you'd be better off pondering the surrealists. Though leave *Un Chien Andalou* aside. Dali, Duchamp, Magritte, Ernst, and the others, had fun with that bugger, reality, asking which vision is all the more real: their version of the world or ours?

The answer to that question is what the rest of the songs in "The Machine Gun Rag" would have explored; meandering and muddling through choruses and stanzas to track the fears, expel the demons, rant, and rave and do all those things lyricists do with words and poetry to get their minds at ease and their world at rest. Those pondered, but not yet written, lyricals; those words shoulda-woulda-coulda-been-written way back then in my formative years, my High School years.

With my past track record of incompletion, I would hate to leave the question unanswered, hanging out there waiting for that micro-opera to be finsihed, let alone have someone put music to it. Or then wait for me to end my procrastinating ways and gather enough stamina to word-process, layout, and proofread the third version of this folio. Then another few months to figure out how to put a new order to the collection only to have it go all alphabetical again.

Then, pray tell, you may ask, whose reality is more accurate? In a word, neither. It's not one or the other, but yours is yours, and mine is mine, and, personally, I'd rather keep mine a little safer...live a little stronger, push into a future holding onto that little something we all call "later." Hmmm, sounds like another chorus to me. Time to get me another set of notebooks to kick the third *Mud Folio* into gear and write me some more lyricals-not-yet-sung.

Although without fully realizing that song, or all the others still unwritten, and with the "Rag" lying unfinished, I still have a little vitriol curdling up in my medium-soy-dark-no-sugar-french-pressed-ground-fresh-water-under-boil-ing -point-perfect cup of coffee this morning, and here it is: Yo, intolerant fundamentalists, all of you trying to downsize the competition and level down the playing field all over this world, or yes, you hooligans right here in the US-of-A hog-tying up our great land of democratic freedoms, you should practice what I remember Max Ernst titling one of his collages; "Watch Your Hat."

Your own hat, terrorist dudes, not mine, not my family's; watch your own damn literal and metaphorical, freaking hat. Then, put it on, whistle a tune of your choosing, and do a little walking hat on a sunny day.

Walk away, hat, walk far away.

About the author

When he first compiled this *Mud Folio* in 2012, David Greenberg lived on Cape Ann in Massachusetts with his brood of Greenbergs: wife, Laurie, two daughters, Mia and Tess, and a dog, Sadie, who waited to bark at real or imagined intruders right when David was about to eke out the perfect quip or rhyme. During the working week, when he was not hurriedly scribbling down ideas before the muse left the room, or walking the dog, making dinner, checking Facebook, then Instagram, he could be found behind his Director of Marketing desk for a music booking agency that was full of the creme de la creme of the jazz world and beyond, but will not be named here, much like Ms. Rowling's Voldemort.

With this second edition, we find Greenberg still on Cape Ann, while his daughters have retreated to Seattle, far away on the opposite side of America from the Eastern tip of Massachusetts. But you should look no further than *work takes them there* as the reason. Or so we're told. They could have moved even further westward into Asia. Or eastward, as Paris has always fascinated. So Seattle seems to be just right, for now.

Though there is a grandkid, Desmond Oswald Heaton. The cutest ever, but all Grandparents say that. Even with FaceTime and texted photos, or because of those, the distance for the Grandparents is still feeling farther these days and nights.

Sadie had added trying to catch flies, real and imagined, indoors and out, to her resume of *barking at things* and was still keeping the Greenberg house safe from intruders, again, real and imagined until recently. After fifteen years, she sadly left this world and is on to the next. Very sadly, as it has happened while working on the first proofing of this version. (We then got busy doing other things that paid the rent.) In time, the memories of that little booger will shine a little brighter instead of obscured behind our sadness.

Laurie has left the industry of salaried product design behind, battle-weary, permanently furloughed, and is looking toward the bright horizon as the storm clouds retreat, as well as to the wonderful smell of oil paints, turpentine, and mineral spirits perfuming the house.

On weekdays, Greenberg is the Director of Marketing and Development for an enthusiastic bunch of people at yet another music booking agency which shall be named: Music Works International. Greenberg loves helping musicians make a good to great living in the entertainment business, helping then find new and bigger audiences to fill those seats for the select few who need that expertise.

It also helps Greenberg stay sane when MWI sends him to far-flung places to help develop the company's audience: Tequila in Tequila was a nice perk, house-boating in Amsterdam and finding, in a stall on a stroll with his wife through Hong Kong's Cat Street, a retro (circa the '50s) statue of Mao smoking a cigar and wearing khakis, and finding a unique bronze Buddha in Singapore were others.

After dusk, most-often between dinner and turning in, Greenberg freelances: designing intriguing items, like the book you have in your hands, or posters for tours and graphics for album releases, or marketing underserved music and musicians as well as creating a bevy of assorted items to the general public that they do not need, but should not do without.

Really. Like this book. And you know your friends could do amazing things with one of their own.

Right?

Oh no, there's more

The first version of the *Mud Folio* was not only self-published but also self-designed. For this edition, the extra sediment edition, I thought I would switch it up and have Nathan Shumaker send the text through his design process, and it came out much differently than the Tape Dave version. Like Hal Freedman's version of "Night Stories," flipping it from what I thought the song was trying to become only to emerge into his preferred genre of salsa, Nate elevated this design to another, better level. And I learned a few things in the process.

Doesn't it look great? I saved some time on that, but even so, it took forever to find the time to finish the book, claim it good enough to print, upload it for publication, and announce to myself, "That's done; let's drink!"

One of the great impediments to commence the final proofing was not only Adobe deleting design access to one of the fonts we had begun with, necessitating a font switch out and subsequent tweaks, but also there was the pandemic. The best intentions seemed to fall into the maw of those days and months; then, all of a sudden, it was years later. I found time for other stuff, but this book? The pages beckoned, but I hid them under the tower of books I wanted to read so I could escape the end of the world.

I was in a dark place and did not want to work on anything with a fully awake brain and handy pen, most notably rereading, editing, and tallying up all the words, so many words, still not sung.

So many.

Still.

Not.

Sung.

Months after the masks fell—by the way, the official governmentally sanctioned date, not the loopy one months before when some felt suffocated by medically approved pieces of paper professionals use the world over, mind you—I finally placed pen to the manuscript and scribbled on the pages, noting where to tweak the words, sentences, paragraphs, and thanks to the font insurrection by Adobe; manually fixed leading between some lines, the kerning between some letters. As I went page by page, some sentences looked to be strangled by unnecessary commas, though which of the, maybe too many, commas? They all seemed just right. Not too many, not too little, but just right.

Took them out.

Put some back in.

Pasted the text into Grammarly and found I was right all along. Mostly right. Although, dear reader, those of you English majors, or just majorly English of the British persuasion, you may be dismayed by some commas seemingly strays and misplaced. If so? Not my fault. That damn A.I. could have been hallucinating again. Or maybe it is my fault, and I put one or two or three back in against the will of Grammarly. Maybe. Though maybe not.

And, of course, deciding whether italic or Roman, ALL CAPS or not, going line by line, paragraph by paragraph, inch by inch.

This whole endgame has been quite a joyride in the park, one as gnarly as that noun crashing into that idiom.

Since you have a printed and bound version in your hands, I completed the task at some point. Or just gave up.

ADDITIONAL COPYRIGHT INFORMATION

Again, as you should be painfully aware by now, unless you don't read the all-important teeniest tiny type representing legalities to which, by having purchased this book, the following is considered binding: unlawfully reproducing, distributing, or otherwise violating the copyright of any of the works within, you agree, without contest, to avail yourself to the jurisdiction of the Federal Courts of the United States of America and perhaps even Greenberg's wife. In other words, you don't want to go there.

NON-EXCLUSIVE LICENSE (TO THRILL)

Herein, to start the ball rolling and get the full-on legalities started—the usual avalanche of paperwork; copyright forms, co-publishing agreeement, and on—is a non-exclusive license to marry a lyric found within the MUD FOLIO with original music.

AGREEMENT ANNOUNCING COLLABORATION
IN AN UNPUBLISHED MUSICAL COMPOSITION
NOT REGISTERED FOR COPYRIGHT

This will confirm my interest to compose music to the following lyrics of David Greenberg as published in the MUD FOLIO and initially copyrighted by Tape Dave Music Co. and David Greenberg:

(title of song): _____

_____

It is understood that this is a preliminary non-exclusive license to begin the collaboration on the above noted works. Additional paperwork will follow upon completion of the work(s). Signing of this agreement in no way constitutes the joint ownership of copyright in the materials or the assignation of rights to a publishing company, or any other person or entity.

Dated:

Signature: _____

Name: _____

Address: _____

City/State/Country: _____

Email: _____

Phone/Fax: _____

Send this form (and all other inquiries) to:
David Greenberg c/o Tape Dave Music Co. 131 Essex Street Beverly, MA 01915 USA